HIDDEN

Millennium

HIDDEN

Millennium

THE DOOMSDAY FALLACY

STEPHEN KOKE

FOREWORD BY DAVID SPANGLER

CHRYSALIS BOOKS

West Chester, Pennsylvania

Library of Congress Cataloging-in-Publication Data

Koke, Steven.
    Hidden millennium : the doomsday fallacy
    / Stephen Koke.
            p.   cm.
    Includes bibliographical references and index.
    ISBN 0-87785-376-2
    1. Millennialism—Controversial literature.
    2. Swedenborg, Emanuel, 1688–1772—Views
    on millennialism.
    3. New Jerusalem Church—Doctrines.
            I. Title.
    BT891.K65   1998
    236'.9—dc21   98-13696
                         CIP

Cover Art: Detail from Last Judgment by Roger van der
Weyden (c. 1399). Provided by Giraudon/Art Resource,
New York

Edited by Mary Lou Bertucci
Designed by OX+Company, Haddon Heights, NJ
Set in Perpetua Roman by Sans Serif, Inc., Saline, MI

Printed in the United States of America

Chrysalis Books is an imprint of the Swedenborg
Foundation, Inc. For more information, contact:
        Chrysalis Books
        Swedenborg Foundation Publishers
        320 North Church Street
        West Chester, PA 19380
        (610) 430-3222
        or
        http://www.swedenborg.com.

                1 2 3 4 5

CONTENTS

WHEN THE STARS RISE
FROM EARTH

by David Spangler

For as far back as I can remember in my life, I have been aware of and connected to the spiritual or inner worlds. As a child I had a number of mystical experiences; and from time to time, I would be visited by very loving and supportive individuals whose bodies were made not of the same flesh as mine but of a softly radiant light. Not having any reason to suspect otherwise, I took these visitations as being very normal and assumed that everyone else had similar experiences of the spiritual worlds. It was not until I was in my teens that I discovered this was not so.

In 1959, as American culture poised unknowingly on the brink of a new decade that would become synonymous for social and technological upheaval and change, my parents and I moved to Phoenix, Arizona. There, we made new friends who, we discovered, were part of an intriguing network of metaphysical and esoteric groups, psychics, and channels. As we became involved ourselves, I was introduced to the prophetic visions and ideas of a coming New Age.

This was a life-changing experience for me. Something in this idea of a New Age spoke very deeply to my soul and awoke in me an even deeper resonance to the spiritual worlds. Contacts with inner beings and realities that had been infrequent before suddenly became more common as my spiritual life became more responsive and alert. In time, this led to my deciding not to become a molecular biologist as I had intended, leaving college, and becoming the "freelance" mystic and teacher of spiritual insights that has been my profession for the past thirty-four years.

But for all that the idea of a New Age proved a trigger that awoke a spiritual energy within me, I found myself at odds with the millennial sensibility that was at the heart of much of the emerging New Age movement. In this wonderful book, Stephen Koke has called this particular millennial perspective the "doomsday fallacy." Bolstered by many psychic prophecies and claims that worldwide destruction was imminent to "cleanse" the earth and make it ready for a new and better civilization, a great deal of energy was spent among the groups and people I knew in the late-1950s and early-1960s anticipating and getting ready for the apocalypse to come. Doomsday was literally at hand; and judging from the recently released Russian and American intelligence documents chronicling just how close the world came to thermonuclear war during the Cuban Missile Crisis, the psychics were obviously picking up on a very real danger and possibility. But my own perceptions into the spiritual worlds consistently failed to see any evidence of a literal apocalypse just around the corner, and my inner contacts steadfastly maintained that the earthly changes and upheavals being prophesied were really inner phenomena that would hit at spiritual, psychological, and social levels. From their perspective, to take doomsday prophecies literally was to miss or even distort the fullness of what was actually transpiring.

In fact, the variance between my own inner experiences of an unfolding spiritual transformation at work and the accepted belief in the New Age movement of those days that a physical apocalypse was at hand put me in an embarrassing situation while attending a New Age conference. I was sitting through a lecture by a local Arizona psychic who was holding forth fairly graphically about all the upheavals and catastrophes that were about to befall us when something in me arose in protest. Much to my own surprise, I sprang to my feet and shouted out, "None of that is going to happen!" There was a stunned silence. Then the speaker shouted back, "And who's going to stop it? You?" to which, to my even greater surprise, I said, "As a matter of fact, yes!" In that moment, I did not feel I was talking on my own behalf or making a megalomaniacal statement of my own power, but instead felt I was speaking on behalf of the compassionate and loving nature of the spiritual world that has no desire or intent to inflict suffering upon humanity in the name of evolution.

I mention this bit of personal history to explain my great delight in reading the book, a delight that is threefold. First, Koke has gathered together in one volume a most informative overview of millennial thought throughout the centuries. Second, he provides an excellent introduction to Emanuel Swedenborg's thought on this matter, something about which I knew very little before I read this manuscript. And third, as my preceding story suggests, I thoroughly agree with the premise of this book and share with the author the conviction that it is important for spiritual seekers to shift a perspective of transformative nature of our time from expectations of disaster to an awareness of the inner changes available to us and occurring around us every moment as this millennium ends and another is born.

There are many reasons that making such a shift can be difficult. For one thing, as evidenced by the box-office success of the successive summer disaster movies, apocalypse has a compelling drama to it. In a morbid way, it is fun to contemplate, particularly since we usually envision it as something that will strike others while leaving ourselves untouched.

For another, doomsday might seem to promise a longed-for salvation from the troubles of our lives. I remember well a woman who came to me for counseling in the mid-1960s. At the time, there were a number of apocalyptic prophecies that had sprung up around the destruction of Salt Lake City where she lived, and one well-known psychic had even written a small book that pinpointed the actual day on which this disaster would happen. When this woman came into my office, she was agitated and in distress; when she described these prophecies to me, I assumed that she was afraid they would come to pass. However, I was mistaken, for when I asked her this, she said, "Oh, no! I want this prophecy to happen. I'm stuck in a dead-end job, a lousy marriage, and I have no prospects for change. I'm afraid Salt Lake won't be destroyed, and I'll have to go on the way I am!"

There are many things in modern civilization that we may dislike but feel powerless to change. Historically in Europe, millennial movements and prophecies originated in and appealed to those who were most dispossessed and had the least to lose if society collapsed. While such a movement can seem like a visionary and creative endeavor, more often it is a refuge for those who feel powerless and lack vision and creativity. The image of society changing through the instrumentality of disasters is in a league with other personal and collective perspectives that see no alternative except violence as a way of resolving conflict or effecting change. As such, it lacks imagination and flexibility.

Paradoxically, for all its talk about a transformed future, the modern New Age movement is remarkably lacking in imaginative ideas on what that future might look like or how it might be brought about short of apocalypse. The really innovative work in reimagining and transforming politics, economics, social institutions, spirituality, science, and technology is largely being done by people who want nothing to do with the New Age, which they see as having collapsed into narcissism and disaster-mongering. And perhaps this could be said about other millennial movements as well. They view the future either like a deer caught by headlights in the middle of a darkened road, fixated upon approaching doom, or like an executioner smacking his lips as he raises his ax over his intended victim, anticipating the death of what is personally distasteful; neither perspective is conducive towards embracing humanity and our tomorrows with a creative imagination.

What is needed, as Stephen Koke points out, is a deeper grasp of our spiritual capacities, as well as of the reality of the spiritual nature of our world. This is important both to help us to move through the thicket of prophecies with discernment and grace and to give us access to our power to imagine and co-create our future.

In the former case, there is a layer of visions and dreams surrounding the earth born from the fears and longings of humanity, and when a psychic opens up to the inner, it is entirely possible to tap into this layer and view what is within it as if it were an image of the future. Indeed, I remember a powerful example of this in my own life when a friend of mine was visiting me from Germany in the late 1980s before the collapse of the Soviet Union. He told me of the fears in Europe that the Soviet army was preparing to invade and asked what information I could gain through spiritual sight. When I looked inwardly, I was astonished and concerned to see waves of Russian tanks rolling across farmland while jets fought a savage battle in the skies overhead. It was a very clear image of a Soviet invasion, but something about it didn't feel right. So after my friend went to bed, I looked again and could see that I had tuned into his fear and had ridden it into the psychic layer where it took the shape that it did. It had been a psychic movie, not a true vision of the future at all.

A dominant feature of this layer of collective psychic images is fear. It reflects little of the love and transformative compassion and joy that is so characteristic of the higher spiritual domains, from which emanate many influences that do co-create our future with our own imaginings and creativity. The fact is that many of our images of the sacred and of spirit are fearful images as well—such as the judgmental God—and thus do not always align us with sources of light beyond the psychic layers of collective unease. If we truly want to touch those spiritual levels and allies that are most concerned with our future, then we need to do so through a discipline of love.

Likewise, if I am unable to love my world and all the people and things in it, then it may be harder for me to summon a joyful creative imagination and a spirit of innovation and action to be an active participant in change rather than a passive victim of apocalypse. Surely that perspective of lovingness and compassion is augmented by a deeper understanding of and attunement to spiritual realities.

Swedenborg grasped this and brilliantly shared his insights and experiences to free people from fear and a literal understanding of the millennium precisely so that we would not see it as an event but as an inner capacity for co-creation and transformation. And that is the message for Koke's book, the power and promise of the "hidden millennium." It is a message of the power inherent in the human spirit, aligned with the sacredness within creation, to shape and reveal a future at the edge of our imagination and hope, yet entirely attainable if we will rise to the occasion.

The book of Revelation speaks of the stars falling to earth in the latter days. In Celtic traditions, there is an interesting image of the "stars within the earth," an image that resonates across the centuries with modern science's findings that the earth and everything upon it, including us, are all made of star-stuff, that we are all fashioned from materials born in the heart of stars. In the poetry of this image, perhaps we can see that our time is not a time of stars falling apocalyptically upon the earth but a time when the inner stars, the spiritual powers of humanity, can rise with new imagination and spirit to light and empower our creative way into a greater future waiting to emerge.

We all love any excuse, any public signal, to make a new start and put our mistakes behind us. New beginnings offer new life, a second chance to be all that we have ever wanted to be. A new start feels like being born again, becoming children again, but this time with all the wisdom of our past available to us. The approaching millennium is only a number on a calendar. There is no reason to think that the year 2001 will be remarkable in any way; but, on certain dates that seem to mark a turning point, a silent request echoes through us and around the globe—Let's live again, and do it all right this time. Let's dream again and make our dreams come true. We have some wonderful ones stored up for just such a time.

We are not without substantial encouragement, either.

Communism has ceased to be a global threat and has virtually disappeared as an influence on the fate of nations. Medicine has advanced to the point where it acknowledges the powers of the mind and is no longer exclusively focused on the body as a mechanism to be treated without attention to the person inside. To make a long list of advances short, many people are building a sense of common identity with humanity all over the globe, not just with the humanity of their own kind and culture. A global brotherhood has begun to assert itself.

It is important, however, to see how these things will finally affect us spiritually. Whatever happens in the spiritual center of humanity determines the course of history. What happens to our religious beliefs sets the tone, the meaning, of events that otherwise are mainly material or social. Therefore it is interesting to see what is happening in the theologies of millenarian movements, which are increasing their efforts to convince people that they must face the imminent return of Christ. The subject of the Second Coming elicits mixed feelings. On the one hand, Christ will appear and claim his creation, but on the other hand, no one wants to go through the end of the world. Even non-Christian psychics and teachers offer visions of changes imposed around this time by spiritual or divine forces. These changes are almost uniformly unpleasant—earthquakes, change in the shape of continents, destruction of great centers of civilization, and the death of most of the human race.

Whatever happens on or about the arrival of the new millennium, it will either vindicate many nonscientific methods of uncovering the future, supporting the purveyors of psychic and biblical prophecy, or catapult many spiritual movements into deep crisis. Some millenarian movements are already in crisis, with too many failed dates for the end of the world already behind them.

One thing will surely happen soon after the new century begins—there will be important changes in the nature of Western religion. There are signs already that the news will not be good for millenarians because there are already many signs of weakness in conventional eschatology, the study of the last days. There are too many loose ends, too much neglect of fundamental questions about the nature of God and about what he would be expected to do. There is also too great a need simply to be rescued from the problems of living in the world, and this pressure compels many Christians to seize upon anything that promises an easy way out of our troubled times.

Outside of the established churches, psychics are the prophets of our times. Israel had a prophetic tradition—out in the deserts the prophets lived in intimate contact with the divine and experienced visions. Occasionally, these visionaries were sent into Jerusalem to instruct the king about God's will. Often the kings disobeyed, and biblical history is full of the disastrous results.

Western society has its own prophetic tradition, though it is not labeled as such. Psychics, the most prominent of whom have been the medieval prophet Nostradamus and the modern Edgar Cayce, warn of similar disasters ahead. But there are questions about what their messages really mean. Given the experience of a genuine vision of the future, do psychics also know how to translate them into real, rather than symbolic, terms? Or are they merely the purveyors of raw material, yet to be adequately understood? Having a vision and publishing it require a temperament or faculty different from that needed to interpret the vision. These temperaments are almost opposite. One is outgoing, good at divulging or spreading the message as it was given. The other is inwardly contemplative, thoughtful, good at analyzing the message. Frequently, two corresponding kinds of people must get involved before the meaning of the vision is settled.

The question of how to interpret prophetic pronouncements is critically important to religion. The question was posed long ago, when the great poet John Milton postulated that Scripture has a symbolic meaning. The idea that spiritual thought is most readily conveyed in symbolic images and terms reached its highest development in the work of scientist and theologian Emanuel Swedenborg in the mid-to-late eighteenth century. The idea was carried on, filled out in the twentieth century, and attributed as well to the myths and legends of various cultures, by psychologist Carl Jung and the American mythologist Joseph Campbell, among others.

In contrast to these contemplative analysts is the long and persistent use of language in Western theological traditions in its most literal forms. In this tradition, if a word is so defined in the dictionary, it is so to be understood, especially in sacred texts. Just where such a rule originated becomes a compelling question, for sacred texts need not actually be literal. They could well be instructive stories, analogies of the soul, or episodes that, like dreams, magnetize us and change the very tone and character of consciousness. But a truism in many religious traditions is that God would not risk deceiving us by telling us things in an unclear language: since he wants to communicate, he would use literal terms. That the psyche, the soul itself, may not "think" in literal terms deep inside where prophetic visions are received and new consciousness is formulated is the striking and unexpected result of much twentieth-century research.

For example, all this has a lot to do with what we may label as God's notion of time. Calendars and dates are very important to prognosticators and interpreters of the prophets. But, as we will see in the following chapters, I strongly believe that God is not looking at our artificially created calendar and erecting specific dates on it; as a spirit, he is most likely looking at spiritual time. God's time comes down not to definite dates at all but to whatever states of mind must unfold before a particular further state in spiritual history can happen. This notion of spiritual time as a succession of inner states in humanity has a pace and heartbeat of its own. It is therefore best when keeping track of any prophecy to look at the psychological and spiritual trends by which things are changing, not material dates.

The notion that there is a system of spiritual timekeeping that can accommodate its own dating system—a kind of mathematics of inner states using days, weeks, months, and years symbolically—was developed most thoroughly by Swedenborg. His justification for this theory was Scripture. His study of the Bible's use of numbers and other basic terms suggested that its authors used a nonliteral approach to the key dates and contents of biblical prophecy. Unlike millenarians who use the Bible to calculate exact dates, Swedenborg interpreted the Bible as symbolic history.

In any case, the evident problems of conventional Bible interpretation and the pitfalls of taking psychic visions and readings of the future literally show that new insights are needed to see our spiritual destiny clearly. Such insights reveal a hidden "millennium" that has not been suspected on any large scale before. That is the theme of this book.

I have divided my examination into two parts. In part one, I revisit the traditional view of Christian eschatology, that of the Second Coming of Christ and the Last Judgment, beginning with the early Church fathers. I next examine the history of some prominent millenarian movements within the Christian tradition and their ideas about the future; within these three traditions—the Fundamentalists, the Seventh-Day Adventists, and the Jehovah's Witnesses—I also examine the problems they raise. Finally, part one ends with two prominent examples of psychic prophecy not necessarily based on the Bible. The statements of psychics are a subject in themselves and have increased over the last twenty years in preparation for the new millennium—or at least for the year 2001.

Part two is devoted to a spiritual philosophy that predates many of the current millenarian movements, but is an interesting and thoughtful combination of scriptural studies and broad spiritual experience. In the visions and writings of Emanuel Swedenborg, eschatology, the study of the last days, became part of a fully developed philosophy that is still one of the most sophisticated and suggestive available. Swedenborg's vision of the Christian millennium is one that offers hope rather than terror, one that sees the Last Judgment as an already completed event.

Before proceeding, let me pose some preliminary problems to keep in mind:

First, the psychology of the millennium is not clear: Could the last days actually be a burden, a distraction for the soul to contend with, forcing it to love God "real fast" in order to be saved, despite the fact that love cannot be a hothouse plant? Certainly, the real need championed by religion is for a sincere desire to change our lives; that would arise from profound inspiration and healing in an environment otherwise free of external pressures, such as the looming threat of an end to everything.

Second, the millennial message itself seems incomplete: Do we even know why the world *must* come to an end? What one may notice about millenarian preaching is that it rarely ventures a rationale for ending the world that does not depend on divine impulse rather than divine argument and a thoughtful assessment of our situation. We are not given a rational case to consider, only the message that the world is doomed, and the most fascinating question has merely been "When?" or often, "When can we get out of here?" Millenarians believe that God has determined that the world is doomed, for Scripture authoritatively imposes the idea. Little is said to dispense with the impression that, although God normally works patiently and well with people of horrendous character, in this case he seems especially arbitrary.

I also offer the intriguing thought that the apocalypse may not be understandable if taken literally, since Jesus' teachings on inner improvement, the natural growth of love of God and the neighbor, on the one hand, and the demise of the cosmos, on the other hand, do not accommodate each other well.

With these considerations, I hope to present the reader with a reverent alternative to the traditional forecasts of doomsday.

I must express my gratitude and appreciation to those people who have made the production of this book as easy as possible. My biggest thanks go to Dr. Jim Lawrence, my old friend and co-conspirator in literary projects, for suggesting this topic for my consideration. He has provided great encouragement all along. Also, many thanks to my first book editor, Mary Lou Bertucci, who kept me headed down the straight and narrow. More gratitude as well to the encouraging voices who pitched in with offers of help and suggestions as the book was going through its growing pains, in particular, Susan Poole, who was ever ready to do what she could. I regret only that I had little to offer that she could put her capable hands on. Also, my thanks and my sympathies go out to Dr. George Dole, who had to read three versions of my two chapters on Swedenborg and seemed to bear up under it without complaint. Nearly all of these people are old friends; and when you have such a literary crowd around you, a worthwhile book idea has the best chance of coming to fruition.

Part One

TRADITION

CHAPTER I

A LITTLE BACKGROUND MUSIC

Millenarian movements occur in response to the enormous drama of the supposed end of the world. With some variations in interpretation, the basic Christian drama is that Christ will appear in the air and gather everyone who has ever lived from the ends of the earth for a general judgment. The faithful will be separated from the evil, and the faithful who have died will be reunited with their bodies; they will then be admitted into the Kingdom of God, where they will be granted the more immediate privilege of reigning with him for a thousand years. The evil will be sent to hell and suffer there forever.

Richard L. Rubenstein has written, "It is generally recognized that millenarian movements are a response to acute social dislocation and that, in our times, the modernization process itself has been the principle source of such dislocation."[1] This sense of "acute social dislocation" results in a feeling of not belonging to the world and its troubles. People

---

[1]Richard Rubenstein, "Religion, Modernization, and Millenarianism," in *The Coming Kingdom: Essays in American Millennialism and Eschatology*, ed. M. Darrol Bryant and Donald W. Dayton (Barrytown, New York: International Religious Foundation, Inc., 1983), 223.

yearn to be taken up into a better world, and the promised Second Coming of Christ reassures Christians that release will come. Furthermore, the promise that Christians have always been granted by Scripture is not just one of release; it reinforces hope with a vision of unimaginable joy and glory with God. The result is often a movement, or an entire new denomination, that concentrates intensely on this vision as a central theme.

Modern millennialism began as a desire to predict the end of the world and the establishment of an earthly paradise in which Christ and his people would reign supreme. The ungodly and unbelievers who seemed so prevalent would be judged—or, in one system discussed in a later chapter, simply exterminated, unable to survive even in hell. The immediate passion was to determine when the final victory, which was clearly predicted in the Gospels and Revelation, would come. If the date for the final confrontation was near at hand in these troubled times, so much the better. But a date was very desirable. Dates make a thesis more substantial and provide a sense of closure. They reduce history to a more understandable story by telling us when and how the story will end. Dates for the faithful were derived from intricate analyses of Scripture, even in very early Christianity, that concentrated on the books of Daniel and Revelation, which provide a fragmentary chronology. Millenarians looked for a salvation that is still promulgated by a defensive church. The Second Coming was going to be very like the dramatic rescue of a few lonely survivors from a dark and dangerous world.

Specifically, the rescue consists of the arrival of the thousand-year reign of Christ described in Revelation 20:1–6.

Then I saw an angel coming down from heaven, holding in his hand the key of the bottomless pit and a great chain. And he seized the dragon, that ancient serpent, who is the Devil and Satan, and bound him for a thousand years, and threw him into the pit, and shut it and sealed it over him, that he should deceive the nations no more, till the thousand years were ended. After that he must be loosed for a little while.

Then I saw thrones, and seated on them were those to whom judgment was committed. Also I saw the souls of those who had been beheaded for their testimony to Jesus and for the word of God, and who had not worshiped the beast or its image and had not received its mark on their foreheads or their hands. They came to life again, and reigned with Christ a thousand years. The rest of the dead did not come to life again until the thousand years were ended. This is the first resurrection. Blessed and holy is he who shares in the first resurrection! Over such the second death has no power, but they shall be priests of God and of Christ, and they shall reign with him a thousand years.

In some spiritual communities, an actual change of worlds has been anticipated—a troubled world will be replaced by a new one that will be happy and prosperous. However, theologies are divided on whether the new world will actually be this one. The earth may be refurbished, or the cosmos itself may be remade.

Millennialism is very old and has gone through some interesting changes since the early years of Christianity. In the early apocryphal work, *II Enoch*, or *The Secrets of Enoch*, Enoch reveals what God said to him:

And I appointed the eighth day also, that the eighth day should be the first-created after my work, and that the first seven revolve in the form of the seventh thousand, and that at the beginning of the eighth thousand there should be a time of not-counting, endless, with neither years nor months nor weeks nor days nor hours.

II ENOCH 33:1

This divides history into eight periods, seven thousand years followed by an eighth and timeless period that eludes definition because it cannot be measured by any of our methods of keeping time. It also suggests somewhat obscurely that, in this last period, history will return to the timelessness it had at creation. Early Christian teachings saw the world as cyclical; time would run its course and then return to the beginning and start again. Both the world and the spiritual side of reality would make this return. The anti-Gnostic Fathers, such as Irenaeus, Hippolytus, and Tertullian, based much of their cosmology on the following statements from Revelation:

Fear not, I am the first and the last. (1:17)

And to the angel of the church of Smyrna, write: "The words of the first and the last, who died and came to life." (2:8)

I am the Alpha and the Omega, the first and the last, the beginning and the end. (22:13)

Irenaeus, in his *Proof of Apostolic Teaching*, section 6, presents a very congenial Creed:

And this is the drawing up of our faith, the foundation of the building, and the consolidation of a way of life. God, the Father, uncreated, beyond grasp, invisible, one God the maker of all; this is the first and foremost maker of our faith. But the second article is the Word of God, the Son of God, Christ Jesus our Lord, who was shown forth by the prophets according to the design of their prophecy and according to the manner in which the Father disposed; and through him were made all things whatsoever. He also, in the end of times, for the recapitulation of all things, is become a man among men, visible and tangible, in order to abolish death and bring to light life, and bring about the communion of God and man. And the third article is the Holy Spirit, through whom the prophets prophesied and the patriarchs were taught about God and the just were led in the path of justice, and who in the end of times has been poured forth in a new manner upon humanity over all the earth renewing man to God.

This is a very optimistic view, compared to what we normally encounter in millenarian movements. First, God creates all things good, as Genesis assures us. He then renews all things at the end of time; he does not destroy the world, only some aspect of its current load of transgressions. The end to be achieved is the "recapitulation of all things," and that is done by coming to earth as a man who tries to heal any remaining divisions between God and man. The end of any cycle is less like a dreadful apocalypse than the coming of spring. The Son of God is very like an emanation of God, not a distinctly separate being, and the Holy Spirit is the ongoing work or energy of divine caring.

There were three possible alternatives, if this concept were to change. First, one could stop believing in a millennium altogether; Justin Martyr, in his *Dialogue With Trypho*, chapter 80, said that many Christians did give up hope. Second, one could turn toward the darker concept of a true end to the world in destruction and trauma. Or third, one could change the concept into one that promised a heavenly community of the saved that no longer had any connection with the degraded world. Augustine (354–430 A.D.) chose this last one.

Augustine denied Irenaeus' idea that the material world was fundamentally just as good as the heavenly one; he regarded the heavenly realm as the spiritual world and the earthly realm as the "carnal" world, a curse. The City of God and the City of the World were independent of each other and opposite in quality. To be admitted into the City of God was to reject forever anything earthly.

Augustine's interpretation dominated the Church well into the Middle Ages. Horrifying depictions of the Last Judgment kept many people pessimistic about their own chances, or just depressed by the concept, but millennialism was too much a part of church tradition to be suppressed.

An interesting question—and one of some debate among scholars—is whether the arrival of the year 1000 A.D. sparked any concern among Church leaders or the general populace. After all, the numerical year itself indicates that an old millennium has passed and a new one is commencing. Richard Erdos asserts in *A.D. 1000* (1988) that panic swept through throughout Europe, doomsday clerics organized communes, and riots broke out in some cities. Given the widespread acceptance of millennial doctrine, it seems logical that there would be some apprehensive stirrings among the population. However, there appears to have been no official recognition of the year 1000 A.D., whether from the Church or the state.[2]

Joachim of Fiore (1132–1202) proposed a new vision of the apocalypse in the later Middle Ages. He drew from some of the early Church Fathers in proposing that human history is divided into three ages, each one characterized by a person of the Trinity. The age of the Father was characterized by labor and work; the age of the Son was characterized by discipline and learning, the sacraments, and the hierarchical church; the age of the Holy Spirit was characterized by contemplation and praise. In this last period, everything in the previous ages would become obsolete, and everyone would become a monk. Everything material is subsumed in pure spirit, and since only monks would exist, his scheme implied the end of the human race. But the apocalyptic drama was also made a natural outcome of history. History would simply evolve this way. Joachim's vision kept the Second Coming from being an interruption of history.

As the centuries passed, philosophies of human nature and society became more secularized. The Renaissance and the philosophy of humanism focused on humanity more than spirituality, although neither God nor the Church was entirely abandoned. Still, the earthly world was slowly gaining prece-dence in art, history, philosophy, and, most pragmatically, in politics. It may have been just a further step downward to the

---

[2]Richard Erdos, *A.D. 1000* (New York: Harper and Row, 1988). Stephen Jay Gould addresses the topic of "panic terror" in the year 1000 in his book *Questioning the Millennium: A Rationalist's Guide to a Precisely Arbitrary Countdown* (New York: Harmony Books, 1997), 80–86.

attempt of Nicolo Machiavelli (1469–1527) to make the paradise that everyone wanted purely a matter of human effort. He wrote:

> *Many writers have constructed imaginary republics and principalities which have never been seen nor known actually to exist. But so wide is the separation between the way men actually live and the way they ought to live, that anyone who turns his attention from what is actually done to what ought to be done, studies his own ruin rather than his preservation.*
>
> THE PRINCE, CHAP. 15

Philosopher theologians, at least according to some people, were aiming too high.

Many writers persisted in attempting to rationalize human hopes. Machiavelli believed that everyone was bad and was ready to prove his contention; a number of prominent thinkers after him taught that the best society will feature a proper balance of the natural passions. Rather than be idealistically good, following the lead of unarmed prophets who were too effeminate to be successful, people should expect to be comfortably self-regarding within a rational civil order, a reasonable trade for a state of chaos. The philosophers who took up this thesis included Thomas Hobbes (1588–1679), who named competition for power as one of the natural passions that could be a legitimate part of civil life; John Locke (1632–1704), who named acquisitiveness; and Georg Hegel (1770–1831), who named desire for recognition. Machiavelli had named fame. All of these are socially useful. They will bring not an ideal goodness, but a balance of powers and a form of prudent mutual respect.

What would drive this society? According to Hobbes in *Leviathan*, the fear of death. That would mean that self-sacrifice, facing a lethal danger for someone else, or martyrdom for a heavenly ideal, would not be expected. Indeed, such an action would be considered unwise. A prudent mix of virtue and vice might be necessary to preserve order in this society.

Although this is only the briefest review of philosophy, such thinking actually typifies much modern social planning, although it is not so baldly put as in Machiavelli's writings. The earlier ideal of society, modeled on a vision of heaven and governed by God or his servants, became demythologized. The secularization of society along these lines is very tempting, because it does not require that one take on the burden of believing in the invisible, the ideal, or the merely hopeful.

With the secularization of society, there came a loss of spiritual vision, and subsequent millenarian movements show the tendency we have mentioned to be grounded in self-preservation, but allowing faith to drift into very literal or material interpretations of history and Scripture. More recently, a kind of technology of mathematics in Scripture came forth as an indirect product, it seems, of the scientific age whose mathematical precision had been giving the religious community so much trouble.

Another element in secularization, particularly in Western thought, is the dominance of rational science. The burdens imposed by our time come from the trend in our culture to put the solutions to problems in some material form. If anything needs to be improved or fixed, some device or technology will do it. The soul, the essence of the immaterial, has had a hard time asserting its existence or healing power in the face of the rise of natural science during the last three hundred years, the influence of Western technology on values and ideals, and the closely related growth of the impersonal marketplace where commodities, marketing strategies, and the dollar are all that matter. In each of these cases, the source of healing, of being enriched, or of the way to get some condition fixed, is something rational, which in our culture means scientifically approved, materially demonstrable, and independent of ancient ideas, the supernatural, or sentiment.

The temper of the last four hundred years has demanded that the pre-scientific past be disavowed. In order to establish the modern objective mind, the world had first to be cleansed of its many demons, ghosts, and supernatural powers. A universe populated by too many of these willful powers keeps physical law from being uncovered and explained, for the actions of someone's will cannot be reduced to law and predicted. Science finally had to disengage itself from religion so that it could define its goals.

Science finally did define itself through the work of many gifted individuals, especially Galileo Galilei in the late-sixteenth and early-seventeenth centuries, Isaac Newton in the late-seventeenth century, and Pierre Simon de Laplace in the late-eighteenth century. Newton established the empirical method, the new way to think about the world, and Laplace, the French astronomer and mathematician, turned it into what has become known as "classical physics," a picture of the universe as devoid of soul but inherently predictable and finally open to the discovery of its inner workings. Certainly, one of the many benefits of classical physics is that it has defined, and thereby created, the objective mind, a major turning point in the evolution of human consciousness.

Classical physics and its models of how to solve problems dominated Western intellectualism until the early decades of the twentieth century when the work of Albert Einstein, Sir Arthur Stanley Eddington, Niels Bohr, and others introduced relativity and the fascinating, outrageous behavior of subatomic particles in quantum physics. New discoveries and theories loosened up the mechanical certainties of classical physics and reintroduced uncertainty, though not as the product of supernatural powers.

Given the trends in Western society and science, spirituality as a religious view of existence was shoved into a corner. It is interesting that the modern surge in millennialism dates especially from the early-nineteenth century when classical physics became the standard model for rational thought. The root of much modern millenarian interpretation in Scripture was the work of William Miller, a Baptist farmer in New York State, who calculated that the Second Coming of Christ would occur about the year 1843. Several significant denominations sprang from it, even after the prediction failed. These modern movements were not inspired by the approach of the calendric millennium—still almost two hundred years ahead—although the millennium always seems to confirm the idea that some kind of rescue should be at hand.

Joseph Mead, a seventeenth-century Anglican, taught that history moves ever upward, and revelation is literal and inevitable. He was the reverse of Augustine. Jonathan Edwards (1703–1758), an American revivalist, taught that Christ's kingdom would come near the end of the twentieth century—one of the earlier attempts to focus on or near the calendar millennium. And the Social Gospel of the late-nineteenth century argued that the kingdom can come now.

Millennialism since Irenaeus gradually dispensed with positive values and metaphysics and became an extension of historical prediction, social reconstruction, and reform, but for increasingly secular reasons as well. Western thought has tried seriously to ground itself as it has never done before.

We must raise questions, as we look in the next chapters into some modern millenarian movements, about whether any of these visions and philosophies has actually been very helpful in improving human consciousness. Irenaeus' ideas remain remarkably appealing as a positive vision of the world and God's actions in it. But his optimism has been forgotten in the gradual growth of a dark and inherently pessimistic view of the world and its future.

p. 6

CHAPTER II

THE FUNDAMENTALISTS

*D*espite a widespread impression, Fundamentalism is not a product of the American south; it began in the northeast United States. The offices of The National Association of Evangelicals are in Wheaton, Illinois; the major periodical, *Christianity Today*, is published in Washington, D.C. The movement began in the nineteenth century as a reaction against what was perceived as the deterioration of the Protestant faith. Societal forces added to a general pessimism—labor problems, social unrest, and huge numbers of Roman Catholic immigrants; the latter in particular seemed to indicate that the American dream was being diluted.

But what gave burgeoning Fundamentalism the most energy was a widespread reaction among Christians to "modernism." The deterioration of the "house of faith" seemed most alarming during the ascent of scientific investigation and the spectacular new discoveries and technological developments it produced. Historical criticism of Scripture arose from a strong respect and preference for scientific analysis and its dedication to facts that could be proven through research and testing, thus edging out the old Protestant tendency to rely on the Bible for a general cosmology and any information about the nature of things. From a modernist perspective, the Bible had to be evaluated scientifically like anything else, and the result was always painful, a fall off the mountain of belief.

Under pressure, believers adopted a kind of counter-science. Literature showing evidence for Biblical statements pitted itself against the skeptics and their findings. But, of course, the new findings in support of biblical truth also expressed the growing trend to elevate material evidence.

Many besieged Christians qualified their interpretations of the Bible somewhat because of the new criticism. What kept respect for the faith very alive nevertheless was the fact that Christianity relied on other things besides Scripture. The church, with its programs and responsibilities, sustained faith, along with the insights and small miracles of everyday experience. Besides belief in the church, there was the central belief that everyone must be "born again." The conversion experience, impressing one with the power of the Holy Spirit, established membership in the Kingdom of God.

In 1878, James H. Brookes, a Presbyterian minister from St. Louis, Missouri, organized and led the Niagara Conference in Niagara Falls, New York. The conference was originally called the "Believers' Meeting for Bible Study," and it met annually for a number of years. Its purpose was to discuss the growing crisis of faith. Brookes presented the following list of doctrines that establish the basic tenets of faith, and most Fundamentalists still subscribe to them:

- *the verbal inspiration of the Bible and the need to preserve it completely from error in the original manuscripts*
- *the Trinity*
- *the total depravity of man*
- *the necessity of a "new birth"*
- *the substitutionary atonement (that is, Jesus as the divine Son of God sacrificed in our place so that humanity would not be destroyed)*
- *assurance of salvation for those who believe in Jesus*
- *the premillennial Second Coming of Christ.*[1]

[1] "Fundamentalist and Evangelical Churches," *Encyclopedia Britannica*, 15th edition, vol. 7, pp. 777–780.

Notice the assertion that the original manuscripts were perfect expressions of God's message. Brookes had spent a year at the Princeton Seminary before his ordination. His statement on the inerrancy of the Bible suggests the Princeton position that the original manuscripts had to be perfectly true, even though the currently published versions of those manuscripts in the Bible might be found of dubious content or origin. That there were signs of flawed or biased reporting by some of the Bible's authors was a contention of the new studies in biblical criticism.

The Princeton Seminary and its theology was established by Archibald Alexander, a man of evangelical beliefs, in 1811. It was essentially Calvinistic but staffed with Presbyterians; its mission was to bring an eighteenth-century rationalism to biblical theology. Alexander was succeeded by his best student, Charles Hodge, who became very prominent in American millenarian thought. Benjamin B. Warfield was also on the faculty, a man of great intellectual talent. The Princeton group fought two prominent influences in theology: first, deism and its devotion to natural theology, the philosophy that theology can be inferred and verified from nature; and, second, the mystical thinkers who tended to make religion vague and insubstantial, not necessarily in agreement with Scripture. Standing between these two extremes, the Princeton theologians proposed a doctrine of inspiration. Inspiration was a definite experience of communication from God, not mystical; it could be validated externally, therefore with a logic as respectable as that of Newtonian science. The Scriptures contained this holy revelation, God's final word; and it was definite and incontrovertible.

The new biblical criticism that so irritated millenarians forced the Princeton theologians to make some defensive adjustments. A defense proposed by Warfield was the argument that, if the documents of the Bible were a bit inconsistent, the original manuscripts were not. As given, they had to be perfect. Forced to defend this idea, Warfield retreated too readily to the fact that the original documents were not available and many had been lost. It was, therefore, impossible to prove that errors had actually taken place. Of course, it was also impossible to prove that they hadn't. Ernest Sandeen writes, "The gravest charge that can be leveled at the Princeton Theology is that it was not so much a theology as an apologetic, not so much an approach to be discussed as a position to be defended."[2]

The similar bottom line brought the Princeton theologians and the Fundamentalists into alliance, although the Princeton group was not especially interested in millenarian ideas; in fact, some of them were strongly opposed to millenarianism. Nevertheless, both groups defended the idea that the Bible is to be accepted and understood first as without error because God wrote the Bible, and he would never give us a flawed document. The Princeton theologians remained a valued background resource for Fundamentalists.

There have been two major concepts of how the last days would proceed. The "premillenarians" believed that evil would grow and finally dominate the world; then Christ would come and establish the thousand-year reign of Christian ideals. That encouraged a thorough pessimism about the future that was to be relieved only by the Lord's Second Coming to set things right. The "postmillenarians" believed that Christianity, not evil, would eventually dominate the world, doing so for a thousand years—the Christian millennium—after which Christ would come. Thus, the two camps differed on what the future would be like and whether a glorious millennium would occur before or after the Second Coming. The premillenarians have been the dominant movement, and we will concentrate on their history. American Fundamentalism has been almost exclusively premillenarian.

Dwight L. Moody (1837–1899), a Protestant evangelist, brought many Fundamentalist groups together near the end of the nineteenth century. Their platform included a strong

[2]Ernest R. Sandeen, *The Roots of Fundamentalism: British and American Millennarianism* (Grand Rapids, Michigan: Baker Book House, 1978), 130.

interest in foreign missions, and they invested evangelical zeal in what was called the Student Volunteer Movement. At the Princeton Theological Seminary, in New Jersey, Moody discovered a group of scholars who were interested in defending the authority and inspiration of the Bible. There followed attempts to oppose biblical criticism and re-establish the authority of the Bible, but by calm argument, using points developed by the Princeton scholars.

In 1902, a definitive presentation of Fundamentalist teachings, soberly argued and based where possible on the Princeton theology, was widely distributed to ministers and laymen under the simple title *The Fundamentals*. It consisted of twelve "pamphlets," each on a separate theme. It had been put together by Lyman Stewart, a wealthy Texas oilman who funded a team of conservative Bible preachers and writers.

By 1914 almost all of the founders of the Fundamentalist movement were dead. The next generation was more adamant, more militant, and also more likely to think independently of their churches—for the movement had always been a grass roots movement, its adherents operating within the framework of their old denominations. In the contentious atmosphere that sprang up afterwards, various groups disagreed with each other as well as with the modernist foes outside. The top millenarian publications, *Watchword and Truth* and *Our Hope*, broke into doctrinal arguments with each other.

When World War I ended, the millenarians met a number of times in New York City and Philadelphia. Finally, in 1919, Charles Blanchard and William B. Riley joined forces to form the World's Christian Fundamentals Association. Riley had earlier steered Chicago's Wheaton College (located in the suburb of Wheaton and later destined to graduate Billy Graham) into the Evangelical and Fundamentalist community. The association was the leading organization for Fundamentalist premillennialism, reaffirming the basic articles of the group's biblical and millenarian theology and declaring war on biblical criticism, especially on criticism that grew out of Darwin's theory of evolution. This group virtually cut all ties with academia and tightened its loyalties to the recently founded Bible institutes. The association attacked the Federal Council of the Churches of Christ in America, a champion of Protestant ecumenism, threatening to leave the council if the decline in Christian values was not reversed.

The association was not able to grow, however; by the end of 1928 it was finished. Modernism continued to gain influence over liberal Christians even though, on the political scene, the United States' rejection of the League of Nations affirmed a value that Fundamentalists also affirmed—a world of nations sharing their sovereignty with each other was a threat to American independence. With this rejection of a type of universal government and obligation, Fundamentalists became more inclined to sink into intellectual isolationism.

Modernism was well established in some Protestant denominations, but not in others. The Southern Baptists were still largely conservative; but the Methodist and Episcopalian churches were nearly all liberal, and serious debate was restrained because of the type of government in these denominations. Debates did break out, however, in the Northern Baptist and Presbyterian churches in the northern states.

In 1910 the Presbyterian church declared the doctrines of bible inerrancy, the virgin birth, the atonement, the resurrection, and the miracle power of Christ to be essentials of faith. Harry Emerson Fosdick, a former Baptist who was later to become a dedicated modernist, delivered a sermon in protest to the growing power of the millenarians in foreign missions, entitled "Shall the Fundamentalists Win?" He was soon pushed out of his pastorate, the First Presbyterian Church of New York City.

The strategy of the Fundamentalist contingent within the Presbyterian Church was to get liberals to leave the denomination. The Commission of Fifteen was formed to prevent a destructive split within the denomination and work out a compromise. The commission decided that, since the Presbyterian church had traditionally welcomed a variety of ideas and convictions, the general assembly did not have the power to decide which doctrines were essential to the church. That destroyed Fundamentalist hopes within Presbyterianism.

In the Northern Baptist Church, the general strategy was to dominate the denomination's annual convention, which was run very like the convention of a political party. The Fundamentalists in the church formed the National Federation of Fundamentalists in 1920; they met before each convention to formulate Baptist fundamentals and work up highly focused strategies to take control of the convention. But when the effort failed to move the convention right away, some of the more militant Fundamentalists formed the Baptist Bible Union. In the 1930s and 1940s, the Northern Baptist Church was left behind by those Fundamentalists who formed the General Association of Regular Baptists. Other Fundamentalists, leaving their old denominations, drifted into other churches, such as the Plymouth Bretheren, the Evangelical Free Church, and smaller Fundamentalist Bible churches and tabernacles.

Efforts to gain power in the older denominations were also weakened by the fact that Darwin's theory of evolution—the one scientific theory that encapsulated for conservative Christians all that was wrong with modernism—was not strictly a Fundamentalist issue; evolution also inspired opposition from non-Fundamentalists, and there were bipartisan efforts to keep the theory out of the schools. This strong common cause, therefore, obscured the special causes that set Fundamentalism apart.

No wonder—Darwin had summed up much of the horrific drama that Christians were facing nearly everywhere when he wrote:

> . . . I had gradually come, by this time, to see that the Old Testament from its manifestly false history of the world and from its attributing to God the feelings of a revengeful tyrant, was no more to be trusted than the sacred books of the Hindoos [sic], or the beliefs of any barbarian. The question then continually rose before my mind and would

*not be banished,——is it credible that if God were now to make a rev-
elation to the Hindoos, would he permit it to be connected with the
belief in Vishnu, Siva, etc., as Christianity is connected with the Old
Testament? This appeared to me utterly incredible.*

*By further reflecting that the clearest evidence would be requisite to
make any sane man believe in the miracles by which Christianity is
supported,——that the more we know of the fixed laws of nature the
more incredible do miracles become,——that the men at that time were
ignorant and credulous to a degree almost incomprehensible to us,——
that the Gospels cannot be proved to have been written simultaneously
with the events,——that they differ in many important details, far too
important as it seemed to me to be admitted as the usual inaccuracies
of eye-witnesses;——by such reflections as these, which I give not as
having the least novelty or value, but as they influenced me, I gradually came to disbelieve in Christianity as a divine revelation. . . . This
disbelief crept over me at a very slow rate, but was at last complete.
The rate was so slow that I felt no distress, and have never since
doubted even for a single second that my conclusion was correct.*[3]

Indeed, Darwin's close friend Thomas Huxley, the chief evangelist for evolution, wrote, "Extinguished theologians lie
about the cradle of every science as the strangled snakes be-
side that of Hercules." Huxley recommended that science
openly declare war on clerics.

Devotion in Fundamentalist churches has always been
reinforced substantially by many services and events, liberally
scattered over the entire week. Rallies, singalongs, visiting re-
vivalists and evangelists on crusades for Christ, church camps,
are all punctuated with endless expressions of love and devotion for the Lord and keep the level of devotion high.
Thoughtful, theological sermons are rare; basically, a sermon
will be an exhortation, not an invitation to think. It must stir
up the troops like a football coach's pep talk at halftime. The
witness of the Holy Spirit is, in some Fundamentalist

[3]John A. Garraty, et al, *The Columbia History of the World* (New York: Columbia University Press,
1972), 957. No original source is given for this quotation.

churches, acknowledged even in the form of glossolalia, speaking in tongues. The soul is not given a chance to let its emotions rest. These churches would be difficult for the contemplative introvert.

The marketing and media skills of the upper echelons of many Fundamentalist denominations, whatever branch of mainline Protestantism it stems from, are remarkable. By employing sophisticated marketing techniques and crowd psychology, leaders aim to raise the level of spirit and to do God's work as they see it.

Bible colleges and institutes, such as the Moody Bible Institute in Chicago and the Bible Institute of Los Angeles, are available to the Fundamentalist who desires a scholarly approach to religion. The Bible Institute of Los Angeles (now known as Biola College) was founded in 1908 by the same people who published The Fundamentals in 1902. These centers also publish, operate radio and television stations, set up conferences, and provide speakers. Wheaton College in Chicago specializes in teaching Fundamentalist views in the arts and sciences. People in various professions can find groups set up especially to serve their areas.

Is modern Fundamentalism a defensive movement that has nothing to do but defend itself against turmoil and change? Not as much as it had been. Billy Graham's great popularity brought many people to conservative Protestantism and also softened the image of the movement. Rev. Graham dressed in an affluent style, maintained a flawless public image, softened the old arguments against science, and utilized the newest technology to get his message across. He limited himself, more than many of his predecessors did, to more conventional sins that any American could understand and accept—the crime rate, the weakness of the family, etc.—warning that God's judgment would come down on wickedness as it had in the past. His high ideals, expressed well within the boundaries of common concerns and avoiding very specialized issues, proved that the basic devotion of Fundamentalism could attract the respect of presidents and institutions. As a result of

Graham's leadership and the prominence and visibility of other Fundamentalist spokespersons, Fundamentalism, with only some reservations here and there, is considered today to be part of the American mainstream.

We have described the philosophical roots of Fundamentalism, but what might be said about its distinctive character? A major point takes us back to the Niagara Conference of 1878 and the major tenets that were accepted at that time.

The list of basic Fundamentalist beliefs put together by the Rev. James H. Brookes brings up an interesting problem. The one inflexible doctrine that makes all the others work as they do is the doctrine that the Bible is literally true. The tenet is peculiar in that it is not found in the Bible, yet it interprets the one source of Christian theology and doctrine, the Bible itself. The remaining tenets are all from the Bible, especially the Epistles. In the face of many different approaches to biblical literature, this one restricts the range of possible interpretations of a passage to a critical degree.

The doctrine of the Bible's inerrancy appears to be the chief doctrine of Fundamentalism, the foundation doctrine that defines all the rest, gives them their look and tone. It is certainly the one doctrine least likely to be changed.

But the origin of the doctrine is not cited anywhere. Where does it come from? Since it is not cited or recorded anywhere in the Bible, it would have to come from some outside source that is superior to, has pre-eminence over, Scripture itself. Fundamentalist theology may, therefore, be based on a non-biblical premise of rather obscure credentials despite Fundamentalism's passionate affirmations of Scripture alone.

The answer to any such doctrine may be that every literary work will be interpreted in the way that reveals the most meaning. As problems with any one approach multiply, we have the right to look for others. It would be very restrictive to legislate how anything is to be understood beforehand. Therefore, the field of possible ways to interpret Scripture should always remain open. This is especially true if the meaning has to do with problems in spiritual growth. The Bible is a religious work, and how it reacts to the search for inner and ethical meanings is crucial. If symbolic or metaphorical teaching is used in a passage, the only way to detect that may at times be to look for some very penetrating treatment of the inner life. An author's actual intentions for the passage, if it should be less inspiring than the proven usefulness of the passage, will seem merely academic in the face of its real interest. Theologians are likely to argue that the author was clearly writing more profoundly than he realized, rather than cut out a deeply revealing interpretation.

In actual practice, both literal and non-literal readings of Scripture have been accepted by Fundamentalists, but the non-literal possibilities have been limited to ordinary non-literal kinds of writing—allegorical or metaphorical—provided they are introduced under the conventional rules of discourse. The deciding principle is the presence of conventional literary cues within the text. For example, if we understand when someone has suddenly started to speak in metaphors or to lay out an allegory, the same criteria should be applied to Scripture. If these cues are missing, then the passage is to be understood literally, as it would be in ordinary conversation. Consequently, the doctrine of verbal inspiration argues that a strict literalism may not be appropriate somewhere, but we can expect God to have intended us to understand his Word as we would understand the speech of anyone else. The "verbal inspiration" of Scripture, therefore, becomes a kind of "ordinary language" view of Scripture.

The argument that one hears now and then from Fundamentalist and other conservative Christian groups is that God would want to be sure that we understand him. Therefore, he would use language as we do, without mysterious inner meanings. However, this idea does not consider the various ways in which a teaching can be understood clearly. In spiritual subjects, one deals with inner realities, and they are often expressed most clearly in the language of the soul. Literal meanings deal heavily instead with material things, external events, such as miraculous appearances or observable disruptions of the world. They come from a language that we use to communicate with each other about conditions outside of the soul. When the soul is to be addressed, the words used may have to take on metaphorical or symbolic meanings precisely so that the meanings will be clear to the spiritual soul. A dream or a work of art understood in its own language makes more profound sense than any mundane dissection of it. Literal renderings will seem unclear because unsuitable and insensitive, reducing the meaning to something more academic, well within our huge common vocabulary of material ideas, concentrating on things remote from the state of the heart. Because a strictly literal view of the most catastrophic visions in the Bible forecasts so much upheaval and the descent of so much apocalyptic force from the skies, it cannot avoid distracting us and turning our minds strongly to our fears and anxieties about merely physical survival. Religion may then dwell in the world as physical reality and physical force.

The clarity of the soul is of more importance to religion than changes in any material situation, for the salvation of the soul is the object of religion. It is more to the point, then, to find God's purposes directed not so much to the material order as to the reformation of the soul. Just how this might be understood will be explored later on.

The Fundamentalist millenarians, looking forward to the Second Coming, regard it as imperative that the prophecies especially be understood literally. Metaphor is not given much room to assert itself in prophetic readings. If a hard-edged literalism were not allowed, there would be no assurance that the Lord was in control of the world. The Second Coming would establish the Lord's power, but that event could be defended beforehand only if the prophecies could be substantiated. That need inspired some detailed attempts across the broad range of millennial Christendom to match literal predictions from the Bible with known events so that the progress of history leading up to the Second Coming could be verified.[4]

Many premillenarians did believe rather strongly that Napoleon III (1852–1870) was the anti-Christ mentioned in 1 John 2:18 who would visit great evils on the world before Christ's coming. It is interesting that their interest in Napoleon went so far that he was actually a great hope to them, rather than an arch-villain to be feared and condemned. They hoped that he would conquer his enemies and run his course so that prophecy could be verified and the Second Coming would soon have to occur. When Napoleon III was defeated in the Franco-Prussian War (1870–1871), that hope disappeared, to deep disappointment.[5] When World War I erupted, it also was viewed by some as a prophetic step toward the evil that should foretell the Second Coming.

Although these events were of interest to Fundamentalists, the main argument in Fundamentalist literature, going back to the early days of the movement, seems to rely on the state of religious belief. Biblical prophecies warned that the devotion of the church—the decline of the faith—would characterize the last days. When modernism arose and seemed so threatening, the Bible was thought to be confirmed because it predicted the modernist, secular world we live in and these assaults against its sacred message. This was felt so strongly that some believed that the last days were undoubtedly going to play themselves out before the current generation was gone.

There is also in premillenarian discussions a tendency to cite only very visible, obvious evils. But those are actually the most likely to be targeted and publicized by high-minded

[4]One of the more interesting aspects of millenarian thought is the urge to predict an exact date for the arrival of Christ on earth, which is discussed in the following chapter. Formal attempts to predict the end date were not prevalent, however, among Fundamentalists. In earlier days any Fundamentalist who attempted to fix a specific date for the Second Coming was mistakenly called a "Millerite" by critics, but basic Fundamentalist views on the apocalypse were not linked to those of William Miller.

[5]Sandeen, 98.

individuals and organizations, as they are today. The most dangerous type of evil is spiritual and deeply internal, but on that account more difficult to detect. It is probably sheer spiritual indifference, ironically the death of any recognition of evil, an insensitivity to spiritual and moral awareness, especially in the religious community, which is obligated to be aware. The outside world which is now, and may have always been, dedicated to materialism, is materialistic by default. The very alarm of Fundamentalists today should be considered by them a sign that the end of the world is not at hand, simply because their sense of mission is still strong.

CHAPTER III

JEHOVAH'S WITNESSES AND THE
SEVENTH-DAY ADVENTISTS

*Picture the scene! The darkness of the Eastern sky is pierced by a flash
of lightning. Christ, the King of the East, the great Deliverer, descends
triumphantly down the corridor of the skies with thousands of His
angels declaring Him the King of kings and Lord of lords (Revelation
9:11–16). The heavens depart as a scroll. Every mountain and island
is moved out of its place. The earth is shaken to its very foundation
and splits apart as the greatest earthquake in history strikes.*

*Horror-struck, the wicked flee from the radiant light of Christ's pres-
ence, crying out for the mountains to fall upon them (Revelation
6:14–16). They have hardened their hearts against the invitations of
the Spirit. The flaming brightness of Christ's coming consumes them.*

*As the earth splits open, Jesus calls forth the sleeping saints (I Thes-
salonians 4:16, 17) who, along with the living righteous, are mirac-
ulously changed. In an instant they receive new, glorious immortal
bodies (I Corinthians 15:51–54). While the wicked cry out in agony,
the righteous joyfully ascend to meet Jesus in the sky.*[1]

---

[1]Mark A. Finley, *Discoveries in Daniel* (Siloam Springs, Arkansas: Concerned Communications,
1994), 167.

This is a quote from a Seventh-Day Adventist publication. But it is the way the end of the world is imagined by countless Christians, not just Adventists. Yet the imagery is more that of myth than of physics and material reality.

Questions hang in midair: What corridors of the sky lead to a spiritual realm, as if that realm were located somewhere in space above the earth? Is heaven really in space? If so, why is the earth moving quickly through the galaxy—might it not be carried away from heaven? And how can everyone see the Second Coming if the planet has a curved surface that would permit relatively few of its people to be within view of Christ when he appears? Does anyone alive know what he looks like? Perhaps the angels give the real nature of the scene away with their wings, though it has been debatable that angels always have them. And why should the good people be only those who are Christian and (somehow) recognize Jesus? What about those who have yet to learn about Jesus and are not wicked? Everyone on the planet evidently has to be either wicked or Christian.

These questions may seem overly mundane, not in tune with the dramatic rhetoric of conventional theology, but they constitute an often needed penetration of religious ideas. If a theology or eschatology cannot answer them, then it has a problem.

Now if this were a spiritual scene, not a material one, it would make much more sense. The descent of the Lord from above suggests a spiritual rebirth, a descent from the higher regions of the soul to earthy or mundane consciousness, which does not ordinarily perceive the divine presence in things. The destruction of the earth and of the wicked, and what is commonly referred to as "the rapture of the saints" (the flight of the saved upward into glory), all look like the inevitable glorification of love of God and neighbor over the love of oneself when the Divine appears in human consciousness to reveal itself as the real power behind our good deeds and highmindedness.

The Divine does cause a sharp increase of illumination and a reordering of values when it descends upon the soul. It is a noumenon that is instantly recognizable as such, for the soul is what sees and experiences it. It is not, like the material scene set forth above, something that could raise questions. It sets the standards for clear consciousness and a perception of right living, the emergence of a new vision of life (the paradise on earth as the improvement of worldly everyday existence or the flight into the higher life). Everything that does not agree with this elevated state is automatically rejected, with great changes (the earthquakes) in the way one experiences life and existence. In short, the eschatological drama looks like a depiction of spiritual experience. It would more closely constitute a spiritual rebirth of some kind.

Most millennialists, of course, do not share this opinion. They interpret the biblical texts that concern the Second Coming and the last days literally, some going so far as to try to determine the actual date of Judgment Day, believing that the Bible contains some kind of mathematical formula that adds up to an end result. And this urge to predict the final days is so strong that it may override the spirit of Jesus' words in Matthew 24:36: "But of that day and hour no one knows, not even the angels of heaven, nor the Son, but the Father only." These movements have invested enormous energy in narrowing down the last days as far as possible. Their efforts tend to cluster around the time of the millennium like a magnet, as if this date could only represent a time appointed by God long ago for some turning point not of our devising. The urge to predict is deeply rooted in the human personality. We have an insatiable curiosity about the future that can run off with us, carrying us to extremes of speculation and imagination despite more patient, wiser approaches. We will encounter this urge in another form when we discuss attempts to penetrate the mysterious prophecies of Nostradamus.

Two prominent millenarian movements that have tried to predict the date of the final days with high accuracy are the Jehovah's Witnesses and the Seventh-Day Adventists. These groups have influenced each other, building a laborious eschatology with surprising mathematical precision.

Until 1931, Jehovah's Witnesses were known as the Bible Students. With an enormous zeal for teaching the secrets of prophecy and preparing for the last days, they grew from a small and unpromising movement in 1870 to a highly energetic two million in a century. Despite their growth, the Witnesses have faced enormous disappointments. An impressive system of Bible interpretation produced dates for the Second Coming and various preliminary stages of the apocalyptic drama, but it failed miserably—several times. The system was revised and reinterpreted, but each time it failed again. According to M. J. Penton, in "The Eschatology of Jehovah's Witnesses: A Short, Critical Analysis," the movement is now in crisis and may not be able to survive another disappointment.[2] The Jehovah's Witnesses are a dramatic example of spirituality given over entirely to its eschatology.

When he was seventeen, Charles Taze Russell (1852–1916), later to become the first president of the Watchtower Bible and Tract Society and the spiritual father of Jehovah's Witnesses, walked into a shabby hall and heard a sermon by a Seventh-Day Adventist Christian preacher, Jonas Wendell. Russell was disillusioned by the Christian doctrine of an eternal hell and was in a spiritual crisis. Wendell's sermon rescued his faith. Wendell and the Adventist Christians had been convinced by George Storrs, an independent "Adventist," that immortality is given only to the saved. Hell, Wendell explained, is not a place but the oblivion of nonexistence.

Russell started up his own Bible study group, based on the ideas of Storrs and another Adventist Christian minister, George Stetson. With that foundation Russell pulled in many other ideas from nineteenth-century Protestant thought and built his own interpretation of Bible doctrines and prophecies.

[2]In *The Coming Kingdom: Essays in American Millennialism and Eschatology*, edited by M. D. Bryant and D. W. Dayton (Barrytown, New York: International Religious Foundation, 1983), 184–202.

One of his conclusions was that Christ's resurrection was not a resurrection of his body but a resurrection of his spirit. Therefore, when he returned before the battle of Armageddon, he would return as a spirit, invisibly. Only the faithful would know of him.

The connection between the Jehovah's Witnesses and the Seventh-Day Adventists continues with Russell's association with Dr. Nelson H. Barbour, who accepted Russell's theory of an invisible return. Barbour had worked with Wendell and Storrs and had been a Millerite. As a follower of William Miller, whom I discuss later in this chapter, Barbour was an unusual Adventist; Barbour derived 1874 as the year of the Second Coming, in which the world would be destroyed by fire. When that year came and went, Wendell and his associates were mystified. But then they learned that the Greek word *parousia*, translated as "coming" in the King James Version, does not always mean "coming"—as in the Second Coming, an arrival—but often and more properly means "presence." That saved the day. The prophecy was restored, as the time of Christ's *invisible* coming. A book, *Three Worlds and the Harvest of This World,* coauthored by Barbour and Russell (but actually written by Barbour) followed in 1877. It convinced many that the mysteries of biblical prophecy and timing had been solved.

Three Worlds uses the year-day formula for the timing of events. According to this formula, so many days in prophecy or in representative scenes in Scripture portend the same number of calendar years before an indicated event will occur. This formula is widely used in American Protestantism. A year in prophecy is also considered to be only 360 days long. The impact of this and other formulas brought in from various Protestant sources produced a satisfying mathematical consistency in both Old and New Testament prophecies.

Barbour doubted Bishop James Ussher's ancient chronology, which had put the creation of the world in the year 4004 B.C.[3] Barbour felt that Ussher's calculation was all of 124 years too *short.* Barbour brought into play another

[3]Bishop James Ussher was a seventeenth-century Irish prelate who had calculated a chronology of Creation derived from the Bible. Ussher's dating system was influential and was often printed in the margins of the King James Version of the Bible.

formula based on one of the Psalms: a day to the Lord is as a thousand years. That led to the argument that six thousand years of history have passed since the beginning, about 4000 B.C. This new reckoning decreed that the world had gone through six "days" and was now facing the seventh, a Sabbath millennium of restitution.

Luke 21:24 tells of the "desolation of Jerusalem," a period during the last days in which the Gentiles would devastate the Jewish nation. Gentile armies would completely surround the city; the Jews would be warned to abandon it and to flee Judea for the mountains.

> [The Jews] will fall by the edge of the sword and be led captive among all nations; and Jerusalem will be trodden down by Gentiles, until the times of the Gentiles are fulfilled.

These events would initiate a period of many troubles, and the great battle of Armageddon, the cleansing of the earth; the return of the Jews to Palestine would follow.

Russell and Barbour felt that it was important to determine how long the "times of the Gentiles" and the time of troubles would last. The result was an impressive synthesis of predictive verses that, although amended since, is still studied by the Jehovah's Witnesses.[4]

A book that influenced Russell's and Brown's thinking was John Aquinas Brown's *Even-Tide*, published in 1823. Brown had dipped rather laboriously into the book of Daniel and reasoned that Nebuchadnezzar was a type of the human family. Daniel interpreted a dream of Nebuchadnezzar's saying that he would go mad for "seven times" before regaining his throne. Before he went mad, Brown believed, Nebuchadnezzar represented the Jewish theocratic government. During his madness, he represented the barbarian Gentile nations; and after he regained his sanity, he represented the kingdom of

---

[4]M. J. Penton, "The Eschatology of the Jehovah's Witnesses, in *The Coming Kingdom*, 178.

Jesus Christ. The "seven times" of his mad years would then be the duration of the "Gentile times." Brown concluded that each of the seven "times" was a prophetic year, which was already considered to be 360 days long. Seven prophetic years equalled 2,520 days. Thus, applying the year-for-a-day principle, the Gentile times would be 2,520 years long. Counting from 604 B.C., the year in which Jewish independence ended under the heel of the Gentiles, the end of the Gentile times and the time of troubles would arrive in 1917.

Barbour revised Brown's argument by starting the count earlier when Nebuchadnezzar destroyed Jerusalem. That brought the end of the Gentile times and the time of troubles to 1914.

Certainly, people who followed the predictions of the Jehovah's Witnesses could breathe a sigh of relief when 1914 came and went without an eschatological murmur, although political events certainly heated up on the world scene with the advent of war in Europe. Russell and his followers got to work and came up with a revised date, 1918. Armageddon would be preceded by the First World War, which would be part of the time of troubles.

Of course, 1918 came and went without the apocalypse occurring. The scholar J. M. Penton reports that the *Watch Tower* of July 1, 1919, spoke with "honesty":

> *Brother Russell was the sole editor of THE WATCH TOWER for many years and made many mistakes, because he too was imperfect. . . . Since Brother Russell left us [he died in 1916], a committee of imperfect men have tried to edit THE WATCH TOWER, men even more likely to make mistakes than was Brother Russell. That these have made mistakes is freely admitted.*[5]

When Russell died in 1916, he was succeeded as head of the Watch Tower Society by Judge Joseph Franklin Rutherford, whose own research came up with the year 1925

[5]Quoted in Penton, 190; *Watch Tower*, 1919, p. 198.

as the last year. In 1918 Rutherford and seven of the Watch Tower officers were sentenced to twenty years in prison for opposing the draft. Another trial after nine months freed them, but the Bible Students were now hounded by mobs and imprisonment, and dissension broke out in the *Watch Tower* offices. All that should come to an end in 1925, Rutherford thought, so he kept his peace. Furthermore, he wrote, "We may expect 1925 to witness the return of those faithful men of Israel [Abraham, Isaac, and Jacob] from the conditions of death, being resurrected and fully restored to perfect humanity and made the visible, legal representatives of the new order of things on earth."[6] However, in the *Watch Tower* of February 15, 1925, Rutherford admitted that expectations for the year were perhaps too much.

Rutherford revised much of Russell and Barbour's work. One distinctive idea of Russell and Barbour was that the 144,000 people of Revelation, chapters 7 and 14, were the saints, the members of Christ's church. The "great crowd" or "multitude" also mentioned there was supposed to consist of a less elevated type who would be admitted to heaven but would not reign with God during the millennium. Rutherford believed that these were a very large class who would live in the earthly paradise. Indeed, many Jehovah's Witnesses believed at this time that they belonged to this class.

More changes were in store. The book *The Truth Shall Make You Free,* published by the Jehovah's Witnesses in 1943, argued that 1914 was the real date for Christ's coming *(parousia)*, not 1874, Barbour's original date. The six thousand years from Adam to the present period were recalculated and said to end in the 1970s. The year 1975 was soon afterwards announced by the Watch Tower Society as the time that Armageddon would be fought. This date was accepted by the Witnesses through the late 1960s and early 1970s.

A series of erroneous dates now exist, and the Witnesses have been ready to admit mistakes and be somewhat apolo-

---

[6]*The Watch Tower*, 1925, pp. 51–81.

getic, if puzzled. They affirm the best motives, the most dedicated efforts, the greatest faith; but these reactions only underline the failures, making them even harder to explain or to embrace. It is easy to feel that it is a paradox that one can have such fine motives and yet be wrong. Revisions to their date theory have been made several times, but the most impressive of dating systems (also largely shared by the Seventh-Day Adventists) has yet to work.

With its theory of Bible chronology having lost credibility after 1922, reactions against the Society's authority came to the surface, especially in France, Great Britain, and the United States.

A crisis of faith had been growing behind the scenes for some time. After 1925 passed without prophetic fulfillment, it became evident that the Governing Body was determined to keep the Witnesses in a state of strict belief. This is shown strikingly in a case argued in British courts. In 1954, the Watch Tower Society's legal counsel, Hayden Covington, testified in *Walsh vs. the Lord Advocate*. Covington was asked by the lawyer for the Crown whether the Society had taught false prophecy when it taught that the Second Coming of Christ took place in 1874. Under further questioning, Covington admitted, "It was a false statement or an erroneous statement in fulfillment of a prophecy that was false or erroneous."[7]

Covington then went on to state that members of the Jehovah's Witnesses were compelled to accept the year 1874 as the date of Christ's spiritual appearance on earth because "we must have unity. . . .[A]n army is supposed to march in step." He further stated that a Witness who disagreed would be "disfellowshipped" because "when a change comes it should come from the proper source, the head of the organization, the governing body, not from the bottom upwards, because everybody would have ideas and the organization would disintegrate and go in a thousand different directions.

---

[7]Quoted in Penton, 196. From *Walsh vs. the Lord Advocate*, transcript of record, pp. 346, 347.

Our purpose is to have unity. . . at all costs, because we believe and are sure that Jehovah God is using our organization, the governing body of our organization to direct it, even though mistakes are made from time to time."

F. W. Franz, then president of the Watch Tower Society and its leading exegete, had said something very similar the day before, though in less jarring terms.[8]

Some Witnesses in the United States and Australia were "disfellowshipped" in 1970 for questioning the chronological doctrine. And in 1980 some senior Watch Tower officials were forced out of the Society's headquarters, the Brooklyn Bethel, after being accused of apostasy.

The roots of the biblical chronology that the Jehovah's Witnesses use is the chronology put together by the Baptist minister William Miller. Miller had been an Army officer during the War of 1812 before his conversion to the Christian faith. Afterwards, he took up his father's Baptist faith. He studied Daniel and Revelation and brought out a chronology of the last days that had an enormous influence on a number of Christian movements. His students were known as Millerites, and they grew in number to about 100,000. Miller predicted that the Judgment would occur on March 21, 1844. When that prophecy failed, he moved the date up to October 22. This second failure led to what is called "The Great Disappointment," and a Mutual Conference of Adventists—as millenarians were then called—convened in 1845 to figure out their problems.

Among these millenarians were Joseph Bates (1792–1872), James White (1821–1881), and his wife, Ellen Harmon White (1827–1915). After reading Daniel, chapters 8 and 9, they concluded that Miller's date, the year 1844, was correct, but that the Lord was not actually supposed to appear to earthly eyes. Instead, the Judgment was the cleansing of the heavenly sanctuary (Daniel 8:14), a prolonged examination of the Book of Life. The pronouncement of sentence and its ex-

[8]Penton, 104, 105, 114, 119.

ecution would occur later. When Christ came, he would come visibly and in person and begin the thousand-year reign of the saints.

Bates and the Whites founded a magazine in 1850, the *Advent Review and Sabbath Herald*, now called the *Review and Herald*. The three founded the Seventh-Day Adventist Church in Battle Creek, Michigan, in 1863. The name reflects their belief that the Sabbath should be celebrated on the seventh day of the week, not the first. They believed that conforming to a sacred practice that was instituted in the beginning by God himself would prepare the Adventists for the Second Coming. Ellen claimed to have experienced revelations, and her theological writings are highly revered in the denomination.

Unlike the Jehovah's Witnesses, Seventh-Day Adventists do not have a date for the Second Coming; they take Matthew 24:36 seriously. Hence, it would seem, they have also avoided a crisis similar to the one undergone by the Jehovah's Witnesses. Despite the lack of a precise date, the Adventists believe that the Second Coming will occur soon and, of course, it will closely match the quote that begins this chapter. At that time, the saved will be granted eternal life, and the wicked will be extinguished—they will not exist. Thus, the concepts of spiritual death and spiritual life are taken literally.

Unlike most millenarians who interpret the Bible literally, Adventists recognize some symbolism in Scripture. For example, the Second Coming is supposed to appear in the East, which is interpreted as an important direction. Darius freed the Jews from Babylon after arriving from the East, and other biblical events (e.g., the wise men from the East who first found the baby Jesus) reinforce the impression that help or wisdom come from this direction. But anomalies like this have not dented an overall literalism that depends on prophecies in Daniel to calculate the birth of Jesus and major events in his life. Carry further prophecies beyond Jesus into our time, and we have a basis for timing the last days—theoretically. Thus, even without an exact date, the Adventists believe that the "signs of the times" indicate that we are currently living in the last times.

Seventh-Day Adventists list the signs as follows:[9]

- *In the material world: earthquakes, calamities, and disasters (Luke 21:11); omens in the sun, moon, and stars (Matt. 24:29).*
- *In the business world: anxiety, economic crises everywhere (Luke 21:25, 26); mobilization and build-up of military forces for war (Joel 3:9, 10, 14); a "peace union" of the nations (I Thessalonians 5:3); international turmoil (Revelation 13:12–17).*
- *In the social world: the crime rate rises (Matt. 24:37, Genesis 6:3); hedonism (II Timothy 3:1–4); immorality in marriage (Genesis 6:2, Matt. 24:37); general immorality (Luke 17:28–30, Genesis 19:1–9).*
- *In the religious world: spiritual visions lost (II Timothy 3:1–5; Matt. 24:12); religious hypocrisy (Matt. 7:21–23); skepticism that the Lord will soon return (II Peter 3:3–5); attempts to "twist" God's Word (II Timothy 4:3,4); only soothing news is accepted in churches (II Timothy 4:3,4, I Thessalonians 5:1–3); religious fantasies are widespread (Matt. 24:24); the restoration of neglected truths (Isaiah 58:12–14); spiritism becomes popular (I Timothy 4:1); millenarian movements react across the world (Revelation 14:6–14); the few who remain devoted are called to stand against these trends (Revelation 12:17, 14:12).*

These signs of the times are too general to point out a particular age, and therefore Adventist (and Witness) arguments would seem to depend nevertheless on biblical chronology; only that actually points to a specific period.

The entire theory of prophetic timing is, unfortunately, a scientific one. That is, it depends on evidence that science provided and is constantly in a position to revise. If it does

[9]Finley, *Discoveries in Daniel*, 155-156.

revise the timing and dates of historical events in Daniel's time, or, for example, the amount of time that elapsed between the lives of Daniel and Jesus, more than one millennial church will be seriously affected. Given a shift in the winds of science, many church doctrines can spin out of control. Churches may then react by making dogma out of their theories, as if to wrest control of their thoughts from science and the tyranny of the current state of archeology or anthropology and make them into divine revelations. This may strike the onlooker as self-serving, since the science that established the original chronological doctrines was evidently good enough for the Millers and Barbours, etc. To abandon the scientific enterprise after embracing it would be arbitrary.

A researcher cannot add a number of years to the date for an event in Scripture and find that another important event will fall into line with the result unless he or she accepts the purely scientific dates already assigned to those events. This is how chronological doctrine works. It leans on science in order to give sense to prophecy and thus gives up its religious soul. The continuing investigations of science will determine its fate, not theologians; that will remain true until biblical prophecy is returned to the realm of religious experience and not identified with our man-made calendar.

That brings us once again to the most widely accepted doctrine in nineteenth-century, and much modern, Protestantism: God meant us to understand him literally. Scripture taken literally is focused on the outer world, and it therefore pulls churches and spiritual movements into scientific territory and eventually into a kind of stalemate whenever science changes its mind. Dependence on science can also be a form of self-surrender for spiritual people. We have seen this happen with the Jehovah's Witnesses, and it was only narrowly avoided by the Seventh-Day Adventists.

When Miller's original dates for the Judgment passed without a murmur from the cosmos, Adventists referred the Judgment to the heavens and the cleansing of the heavenly sanctuary. Was that a legitimate move, or was it a lunge for sanctuary, a way to salt the doctrine away where it could not be refuted? It was not a clean victory. The idea of a heavenly examination of the Book of Life has no validation in our spiritual experience. It is entirely removed from our spiritual dramas and must be taken very dogmatically, if Daniel 8:19 remains a literal statement. Its only evident benefit is that chronological doctrines would have had to be painfully revised or abandoned if the idea of a heavenly Judgment had not occurred.

The future of conventional eschatology is insecure. Inheriting a literal mind and taking it for granted, we allow everything else in modern millennialism to follow, including allowing the changeable sciences to determine covertly the course of biblical studies.

Science specializes in material realities, and literalism about the work of prophets and what they describe makes a church move onto thin ice; literalism leans toward material realities. Science, as the study of mundane or everyday reality, therefore occupies the literal stage along with biblical texts taken literally. Biblical texts then must pose very often as an alternative science. When the Bible speaks of the creation of the world in six days, this looks very much like another science in competition with the formal sciences. And then people must choose which literal account of the material world to believe. The endless wrangles that result are tiresome, uninspiring, and usually unproductive. There has to be a better, clearer, outcome for theology.

In recent times we have seen theories of other kinds spring up about how language was used in ancient times, but they have not had much of an impact on mainline Protestantism. The theories of Carl Jung and Joseph Campbell, profound students of the language of myth, present an entirely different concept of how language has been used in societies not inclined to develop science and technology. These constitute most of the societies of the world. Only in the West has science and its literalism—the use of language for scientifically objective observation and characterization—driven an entire culture. It is now the only way in which language can credibly be used, as far as most people in our culture are concerned.

But religion is in particular not a physical experience; and prophetic texts are therefore most likely not scientific observations of an objective world whose times and dates can be put on the calendar. What drives these ancient texts is the meanings they have for the person undergoing deep changes in consciousness. The concept of time that is involved is most likely psychological, not physical.

One other observation is suggestive. Millenarian movements regard the Lord's coming as joyous news for *them*. They do not consider how good it may be for others still outside of the Christian community who would still need a chance. The Lord is coming soon; won't it be *glorious* when he arrives? Cheers and shouts of "Amen!" ripple through many congregations, as they did in a Seventh-Day Adventist seminar on the book of Daniel that I attended.

For the saved, it is very joyous and fulfilling. But it looks too much like the feelings that people in an enemy prison camp would have when they are about to be liberated. The good guys are inside, looking for deliverance. The bad guys are evidently anyone outside. For all intents and purposes, only Satan's minions are considered to be out there, hounding the community of the saints for whom alone Christ will come. The question of what the Lord must still want to do for the rest of the human race is forgotten. It is forgotten that as long as anyone is still alive in the body, he or she has a chance to reform and lead a new life. Divine love cannot abandon the effort to take advantage of every last chance that such a person has.

Indeed, why impose an end to history? The justification for this immense drama is unclear. Can God's efforts to struggle endlessly with humanity continue at all effectively if the Lord imposes a judgment on still unforgiven sins at a particular date? Such thinking is inconsistent with a Jesus who so loved the world that he gave himself up on the cross for our sins. Now, in millenarian scenarios, we must assume that God is still creating children for millions of expectant parents all the way up through the final hour. Yet these last births will have no chance to find salvation. At least we find that not much thought is given to these loose ends in eschatology.

It may take many failures of literal readings of prophecy to show that this way of understanding prophecy must give way to the consideration of other concepts of language. The failures of Jehovah's Witnesses' predictions, and earlier of William Miller's date for the Judgment in 1844, look not like embarrassing episodes in the history of millenarian thought so much as needed lessons in how to read spiritual texts. If Christian thought has gone this far off track, then revisions must be made in some basic assumptions quickly, for the good of all concerned.

From millennial movements, we go to the predictions of psychics. They too are involved in the millenarian drama and fill bookshelves with commentary on the last days. Two interesting examples of how post-biblical spiritual experience brings about complex questions and new dramas are the works of Nostradamus and Edgar Cayce.

CHAPTER IV

NOSTRADAMUS

He was a little under medium height, of robust body, nimble and vig-orous. He had a large and open forehead, a straight and even nose, gray eyes that were generally pleasant but that blazed when he was angry, and visage both severe and smiling, such that along with his severity a great humanity could be seen. . . . His mind was good and lively, understanding easily what he wanted; his judgment was subtle, his memory quite remarkable. By nature he was taciturn, thinking much and saying little, though speaking very well in the proper time and place: for the rest vigilant, prompt, and impetuous, prone to anger, patient in labor. He slept only four to five hours. He praised and loved freedom of speech and showed himself joyous and facetious, as well as biting, in his joking. He approved of the ceremonies of the Roman Church and held to the Catholic faith and religion, outside of which, he was convinced, there was no salvation. . . . [H]e engaged willingly in fasts, prayers, alms, and patience; he abhored vice and chastised it severely.[1]

[1]Jean-Aime de Chavigny, quoted in Peter Lorie, *Nostradamus: The Millennium and Beyond* (New York: Bell Publishing Co., 1982), 12.

44

We now move to two chapters that present an approach not built from doctrines about the final judgment of the world but that are extracted from the large realm of psychic explorations of the future and the conditions of people and cultures. Psychics are like the prophets who informed the religious cognoscenti, especially in the Old Testament. They receive and publish the *prima materia* that churches may later pick up and turn into more mundane descriptions of divine action. There have always been these two traditions, the ecclesiastical and the prophetic; and although we do not now think of it this way, we continue to have our prophetic tradition.

Sometimes these prophets are honored by the Church, but usually not. Nostradamus' place in prophetic history is controversial. He is enthusiastically celebrated in places, and his prophesies have lately been a frequent subject of colorful media presentations and equally colorful books. However, outside of the inherent drama that the media can mine, he is ignored. He is the most dramatic *and* mysterious of Western prophetic figures.

Nostradamus is the Latin name of Michel de Nostradame, born in 1503. He lived in the little town of Salon, Provence, in southern France, a man of many widely varied talents who saw two great turning points in European history. The Protestant Reformation was underway; Martin Luther had posted his 95 theses to the door of the castle church of Wittenburg when Michel was fourteen, and the Renaissance was redirecting the tastes and culture of medieval Europe. He was a doctor, a cosmetician, a confectioner, a very competent historian, an astrologer, and a clairvoyant.

The Roman Catholic Church was the dominant force in Europe spiritually, politically, and militarily. The Spanish Inquisition was ready to defend the faith rather viciously at the drop of a poorly worded sentence, and astrology was considered to be potentially an enemy of the Church because of its apparent ability to challenge God's knowledge of the universe. Nostradamus' grandfather had taught him Greek,

Hebrew, and Latin, and trained him in a version of astrology that recognized Copernicus' heliocentric picture of the solar system, a viewpoint that would seriously disrupt Galileo's relationship with the Church a century later. Michel early on was aware of his clairvoyant abilities but had to be careful about showing them, since the mysticism that they implied was likely to attract the attention of the Inquisition. The highly placed figures in his prophecies were also not likely to appreciate his abilities; he had to be careful, especially when he was brought to Paris to advise Catherine de Medici, as a prophet and cosmetician (according to Peter Lorie, one who mixes and/or applies cosmetic cures) for a powerful political group. As if all this were not quite enough, he had been born a Jew— although he became a devout Catholic—and he was trained as an alchemist.

The bubonic plague was everywhere. As a doctor, Nostradamus moved with great risk to his own health among its victims, helping people as well as he could, sometimes with unusual remedies. He would gather thousands of rose petals, dry and crush them, pack them into capsules, and place a capsule under a victim's tongue. The petals would gradually release vitamin C into the sufferer's mouth, helping to fight the disease. Nostradamus was so successful with this remedy that he built a strong medical reputation, gaining favor among highly placed dignitaries. But the plague eventually took the lives of his wife and both of his children. He had helped or cured many others, but he strangely could not cure his own family; they had died right in front of him.

That domestic tragedy was too much to bear, and too much for his patrons and in-laws to understand. Nostradamus lost his reputation, his wife's parents sued him for repayment of her dowry, and the local arm of the Inquisition began to reach out for him, threatening to investigate him for malpractice. He gave up his practice and wandered aimlessly in France and Italy for six years. That crisis became the central turning point of his life. After the six years of emptiness and lack of purpose, he began to write his famous twelve-volume work of prophecy, *The Centuries*.

The Centuries contains 965 verses or quatrains, setting out his prophecies for all kinds of subjects thousands of years into the future. They are not easy to interpret, but the very first may be the simplest:

> *At night, studying alone in a secluded place, and rested on a bronze chair, a small flame comes out of the solitude and brings things to pass [predictions] which should not be thought vain.*

This has been greatly overworked by some interpreters straining for a remote symbolic meaning; but it is startling in its similarity to Emanuel Swedenborg's simple experience of seeing a small flame as he was writing his anatomical works. We will discuss Swedenborg later. Nostradamus may just be describing what he saw, a vision that told him, as it told Swedenborg, that he was being illuminated. In other places Nostradamus is very hard to interpret, with his obscure text; his interpreters have run into complications as they try to disentangle his stream of images. Peter Lorie, in *Nostradamus, the Millennium and Beyond: The Prophecies to 2016*, unintentionally illustrates many of the pitfalls that occur when attempting to interpret Nostradamus' prophecies. For example, the following quatrain, with its apocalyptic imagery, has been mined for clues:

> *Mabus then will soon die, there will come a horrible defeat for people and animals: then suddenly one will see vengeance, hundred, hand, thirst, hunger, when the comet will run.*

Lorie attempts to find out who Mabus is. There was a painter, famous in Nostradamus' time, named Mabuse. He took the name from the French town Maubeuge, where his family lived, which means "the bad place." In his interpretation of the quatrain, Lorie substitutes "the bad place" for "Mabus" and states that, applied to the end of the current millennium, this prediction names the entire world as the bad place because of its enormities of war, pollution, and so on, which kill people and animals. Such an interpretation constitutes two steps of removal from a straightforward reading, as well as some dependence on already well-known facts. Why should the name *Mabus*, which is not Mabuse or Maubeuge, really mean "the bad place" when it appears to be more closely related to the painter's family name than to his place of residence? Too many indirect connections occur, and they can only end up with some one of many possible interpretations. "The bad place" then becomes the entire planet, a rather liberal expansion of the normal idea of *place*. The interpretation is driven by well-known modern threats to the environment, not by insight into Nostradamus' method per se. The interpreter takes information that he already knows and merely fits the verse to his interpretation. This is a problem with the interpretation of most enigmatic prophecies, clothed as they are in symbolism and poetic imagery.

To reiterate common knowledge makes any prediction superfluous, not informative, to us, therefore a useless effort on Nostradamus' part. The challenge in interpreting revelatory work is to be prophetic, unexpected, as the prophecy itself was supposed to be. We are supposed to be told things we do not already know. But then there are enormous difficulties in interpreting a prediction and coming up with the incalculable new fact if the author's method is unknown. This problem stalks Nostradamus' work constantly.

The rest of the verse gets no illumination in Lorie's book: *one will see vengeance, hundred, hand, thirst, hunger, when the comet will run.* Certainly, there is a lot here, equally mysterious and not necessarily at all familiar as more of our culture's already tiresome problems. What is *hundred* or *hand,* or even *the comet?* What remains very possible is that the decoding of these items will force a revision of the entire interpretation.

This verse is readable, but so often Nostradamus' quatrains don't even make sense as literary metaphors. Metaphors at least take place in grammatical sentences. Nostradamus played very loosely with all aspects of writing.

Later, in his interpretation, as we shall see, Lorie goes on to astrology, tying things down with an interpretation of a powerful astrological conjunction in our time. What is interesting, again, is that the astrology could have done the same work as the interpretation, with the exception of the final line. Astrology, as we will see later in this chapter, is the formal system in the loop, whereas the quatrains are not. It should, in a pinch, outrank the mysterious verses as the main source of ideas.

> *Flowers [or* pestilences *in old French] passed, reduces the world, for a long time peace inhabits the lands: people will travel through and embrace the sky, sea, and land: then wars will start up again.*

Lorie, recalling Nostradamus' flower-based cure for the dreaded bubonic plague, believes that this prediction can be dated by looking at the line, "people will travel through and embrace the sky, sea, and land." This, he contends, points to a time when we will be familiar with all forms of travel and therefore indicates the modern era. Further, "together with other clues in the verse, [this] points to the 1960s. Nostradamus' reference to the flowers (or flower power) of the 1960s, a delicate power to heal mankind after the terrors of the World Wars, confirms the timing."[2]

Well, maybe so, maybe not. This is very imaginative thinking filled with both clever and stretched points. How many candidate scenes in history have to be passed over in order to arrive at this one? Details go begging. When was there nothing but peace? The war in Vietnam was a focal point for the flower children of the 1960s. The verse suggests that

[2]Lorie, 58-59.

entire populations—"the lands"—are very peaceful, not a mi-
nority group staging peaceful protests in a troubled nation
that had little sympathy with flower children. The onset of war
in the quatrain afterwards suggests that the general peace
broke down. But that, too, is subject to anyone's interpretation, if only because it postulates an unmeasured period between this peace and the beginning of war. One can divide all
of history into periods of war succeeded by periods of peace,
which were, in turn, always succeeded by periods of war, and
so on. This part of Lorie's interpretation lacks specific references that describe an actual time. It depends, therefore, on a
vague philosophy that describes the peaceful embrace of the
planet. But we have yet to see any such era.

As I mentioned earlier, Lorie then reverts to astrology to
help nail down his interpretation. There was a conjunction of
Uranus and Pluto in Virgo in the 1960s, an astrological occurrence that supposedly indicates a time of radical change in the
way that people conduct normal life. But how this upheaval
manifests itself is open to various levels of interpretation in astrology, ranging from external changes (new technology, the
development of nuclear energy, etc.) to deeply internal shifts
in consciousness and ideals that may have nothing to do with
technology.

What is important here is that astrology is the only part
of the predictive process, when dealing with Nostradamus'
work, that proceeds according to known rules. Its hierarchy of
various scenarios, from the most internal to the most external, can at each level be quantified and connected logically
with further conclusions. Nostradamus' prophecies cannot be
decisively pinned down or systematized in any relationship to
real events without knowing his use of metaphor. Is the real
star in Nostradamus' work astrology, not Nostradamus? This is
a question to keep in mind when reading the literature.

I may seem to have dwelt too long and too harshly on
Peter Lorie, but the main point is that all of Nostradamus'
quatrains have this incoherence embedded in them, thus leaving them open to a variety of possible, even reasonable,

interpretations. The field does seem to be in disarray, though it is a fascinating disarray. As the opening quotation from Jean-Aime de Chavigny suggests, Nostradamus appears to have been a sincere and intelligent man who was in the grip of unusual experiences. We will see more of his character below. The combination of the man and his material creates both fascination and frustration.

We all have a tendency to think that when a theory does fit the facts—or when an interpretation does fit the mysterious words—we have the correct explanation and can stop looking for answers right there. But as is taught in the philosophy of science, there is an indefinitely large number of theories that will fit or explain any given body of facts—or words in a quatrain. Concrete evidence is needed to decide between the competing interpretations. In Nostradamus' case, we need definite information on how he thought and how he interpreted some of his own quatrains. It would be something like our recovery of the Japanese code book during World War II. We need to get further into his mind and see what happened. Otherwise, we have the equivalent of an exhibition of abstract art. Any two art critics can bring a crowd through the museum and reasonably interpret the paintings, even if they violently disagree with each other.

At this point, it might seem that we are deadlocked. However, as I suggested before, astrology—specifically the modern use of astrology—may be more of a prophet than Nostradamus. If Nostradamus cannot add to an astrological reading with *independent* information derived from his statement alone and allowed to be strictly revelatory, his interpreters are left with only his vague clues that suggest a general period. In order to pinpoint a specific era based on quatrains from *The Centuries*, the interpreter must employ his or her knowledge of current life and the more systematic rules of *astrological* interpretation. Nostradamus so often ends up as only a dramatic signpost that interpreters recognize only after reading the astrology.

Of course, what one would wish for is more solid direction from Nostradamus himself. He did not want to be clear, however, for he realized that people or governments who were the objects of his predictions could put his life in danger. He even scrambled the chronological order of his predictions so that a ruler or the leaders of the Church could not be sure just where to find a prediction about themselves.

How, then, can Nostradamus be understood? Writing in 1555 to César, a son who was born some time after the death of his first family, Nostradamus tried to explain what his work was about. César would inherit his father's work, and he needed to know how to understand it. He told César that "the key to the hidden prediction that you will inherit will be locked inside my heart."[3] He was afraid not only of the injustice of the time but of "most of the future."

> *I will not commit it to writing, since governments, sects, and countries will undergo such sweeping changes, diametrically opposed to what now obtains, that were I to relate events to come, those in power now—monarchs, leaders of sects and religions—would find these so different from their own imaginings that they would be led to condemn what later centuries will learn how to see and understand. Bear in mind also our Savior's words, "Do not give anything holy to the dogs, nor throw pearls in front of the pigs lest they trample them with their feet and turn on you and tear you apart,". . . so that some human change which may come to pass shall not unduly scandalize delicate sensibilities. The whole work is thus written in a nebulous rather than plainly prophetic form.*

The predictions themselves were the result of astrological calculations and divine inspiration, "the heavenly bodies and the spirit of prophecy." That would suggest that Nostradamus used astrology as a foil for intuitively tuning in to an event or location whose astrological chart he was examining.

[3]Quoted in Jean Charles de Fontbrune, *Nostradamus: Countdown to Apocalypse* (New York: Holt, Rinehart, and Winston, 1980), xx.

If one can calculate or look up the future positions of the planets, a chart for that time can be cast for any place on the globe. Knowing what the chart told him, he could theoretically go into highly intuitive states and sense a lot more than he could had he relied only on his prophetic vision. Nostradamus also mentions spending time in trance. He felt divinely led, not just absorbed with his own powers.

Detecting the meaning of a quatrain would be a very forbidding task for his son or anyone if Nostradamus were going to "lock" its secret in his heart. His letter to César is almost as obscure as his quatrains in places, but he leaves the impression that he required almost as intuitive a process in his future interpreters as he used in composing his verses. *The Centuries* is aimed really at the twentieth century. Nostradamus saw events coming to a head at the end of the second millennium. He seems to feel that, by the time this pivotal century arrived, there would be enough clear connections between events and verses already fulfilled that an interpreter could get a good feel for the relationship between the two. Then with this background, the twentieth century would be ready to read his still unfulfilled prophesies, whereas his contemporaries, lacking this background, could not.

Such an undertaking would, of course, require very sensitive thinkers, in tune with more than their own favorite causes and movements, and able to get above their own century and their roots in it. That is a big requirement, and it is not clear that it has been met. Bringing the magnetic figure of Nostradamus over to one's own side politically and philosophically can be a temptation fatal to Nostradamus' reputation and his intention. The results should also not look like a lot of the literature about his work already out there—overworked intellectual solutions, too clever by far, too imbued with the century's own needs to be strictly rational, even if in favor of parapsychological realities, and favoring current causes that we already know much more about than he did. If we do not manage to project our own favorite causes into the quatrains, the alternative for us is usually an old vulnerability to supernatural authority and suggestiveness. Nostradamus often suffers the indignity of being made into a cult figure. He does not seem to be deserving of such a fate.

Therefore, keeping everything clear and in balance can be a tall order. If Nostradamus was a genuine prophet inspired by higher powers, the fact would very probably mean that the better states of consciousness that our age is supposed to experience may be the only ones able to decipher the predictions. Something similar to Nostradamus' state of mind would be the only one able to properly "feel" into his text and uncover its facts. One would have to rise to his level of consciousness. Ordinary academic, political, or rationalistic thought would be inadequate because too mundane in character, too commonplace, too bound in collective beliefs and controversies to achieve a deep understanding of history. To see the future well enough to justify Nostradamus' claim of divine inspiration and make that inspiration *necessary* may require inspirations that are not about ordinary things. Ordinary events—wars, earthquakes, etc.—easily miss the point that what is required of man is not so much his already well-informed attention to external events but attention to internal ones. As we have seen, spiritual trends are what matter the most, not who is going to be conquering one's town in a few decades or centuries, or what kind of government will reign in London or Washington. Western involvement with the merely literal and material misses the point in scriptural prophecies, and it will probably miss the point in the work of any genuine prophet who had some help from above.

Elijah had an inner breakthrough when he experienced the fire, the earthquake, and the great wind, but then heard the still, small voice that threw him on his face (I Kings 19:11–13). Some kind of *recognition of inner meaning* would be most appropriate to Nostradamus' mission. It is by nature not knowable by ordinary thinking and requires sheer elevation of mind.

Toward the end of his letter, Nostradamus summarizes the last days:

But my son, lest I venture too far for your future perception, be aware that men of letters shall make grand and usually boastful claims about the way I interpreted the world, before the worldwide confla- gration which is to bring so many catastrophes and such revolutions that scarcely any lands will not be covered by water, and this will last until all has perished, save history and geography themselves. This is why, before and after these revolutions in various countries, the rains will be so diminished and such abundance of fire and fiery missiles shall fall from the heavens that nothing shall escape the holocaust. And this will occur before the last conflagration [1999]. For before war ends the [twentieth] century and in its final stages [1975–99] it will hold the century under its sway. Some countries will be in the grip of revolution for several years, and others ruined for a still longer period.[4]

This continues the general trend we see elsewhere to- ward great physical catastrophe in psychic visions of the last days of the second millennium. We will discuss these in the last chapter, for they deserve some clarification of their per- sistent involvement with tragedy. Psychic predictions about our time have not been happy. A golden age, Nostradamus continues, will then follow the return of a powerful monar- chy. That age will be a happy, peaceful era dominated by Sat- urn (order) in the astrological charts of the period. This idea would seem to suggest the biblical predictions of the thou- sand-year reign of Christ, of which Nostradamus, a devout Catholic, certainly knew.

It is interesting that Nostradamus leaned on Scripture as one of his sources. He indicates in his letter that the usefulness of an outside rational source—astrology, for example—is that it allows the mind of the prophet to be free of any "sickness of the mind" which may ensue if only the inner psychic experi- ences were to dominate his or her work. The brain must still work with some sense of conscious method and stay awake. A divine or angelic light also protects the prophet, but from

[4]Fontbrune, xxv-vi. The bracketed material is inserted by Fontbrune.

fantasies that would be imposed by "various nocturnal apparitions." Consequently, "with daily certainty," Nostradamus prophesizes through "the science of astronomy, with the aid of sacred prophecy. . . ."[5] Biblical prophecy seems indicated here as a third protection against getting lost in the nether regions, the catacombs, of what we now call the *unconscious*. Nostradamus confirms his calculations by finding that they agree with "revealed inspiration." Then he quotes from the Bible, "I shall punish their injustices with iron rods, and shall strike them with blows."

Liz Greene, a Jungian psychoanalyst and astrologer, who contributed introductory essays to both Lorie's and Fontbrune's books, suggests that the imagery of Nostradamus' prophecies should not be taken too literally. In Greene's insightful Jungian reading, the great physical catastrophes can signify disruptions of old lands in the soul. The coming of a great King can be "the inner King, the symbol of the Self, the great man within each individual who represents the essence of one's individual life meaning."[6] In Jungian psychology the language of the unconscious, in which such images appear, is symbolic, not to be taken literally.

Nostradamus, on the other hand, appears to have taken his images very literally himself, which is usual with psychics. Psychics may know more about how to have their experiences than about how to analyze them. This appears again and again in psychic literature. The ability to interpret correctly does not automatically come with seership.

This writer has some experience with that. I have had several psychic readings about my future, but none has turned out to be accurate literally. The idea that the imagery is symbolic has been a surprise for the psychics as well as a pointed reminder to me. The psychic is talented (I try to be discriminating) but turns out to be a literalist like almost everyone else. The need to relieve uncertainty with plain factual

[5]Fontbrune, xxiv.

[6]From Greene's introduction to Fontbrune, xi.

information is very strong; one wants real news from a psychic, not puzzles. And the psychic believes that he or she is giving accurate, factual information.

Why would astrology have any part in Nostradamus' work? It is the target of much criticism itself.

According to astrology, we are entering the Aquarian Age, an astrological concept based on the "precession of the equinoxes." The Earth wobbles very slowly on its polar axis, and that axis, extended out to the stars, will very soon move out of the sign of Pisces and into that of Aquarius. The precession through astrological signs moves backward through the signs; normally, Aquarius precedes Pisces. There are twelve of these ages, one for each sign (not constellation) of the zodiac (the sun's path), and each lasts roughly two thousand years. A sign in astrology is always thirty degrees of the zodiacal circle. A constellation is a more adventitious pattern of stars that may sprawl over very much more than thirty degrees, depending on how the ancients chose to anchor their images of the great seasonal periods by the bright stars that happened to lie in the sun's path. Defining the constellations through which the sun would move was evidently their way to convert the sky into a kind of guidebook of the seasons. The constellations were permanently projected into the sky for convenience in reading, even though the stars themselves do not follow these images exactly. The sun's movement through the constellations was a pointer that indicated the current part of the yearly cycle.

Astrologers, evidently noticing that the seasons also resembled certain basic stages in psychological and spiritual processes, decided that a division of the sun's path into twelve equal signs would be less dependent on arbitrary star patterns and more revealing of the detectable nature of things both inside and outside of us. The number twelve has always had great significance in myth and religious prophecy.

The shift by the polar axis away from the Piscean Age is regarded as a shift away from magical, impressionistic thinking, the rule of unfounded mystical concepts, to a more scientific clarity. The Aquarian Age, astrologers theorize, will make us value the individual more for his or her capacity for intelligent, considerate, and logical decision making. Human consciousness has, of course, been preparing for some time now to make this shift. Old unquestioned dogmas have been challenged, and individuals are much more passionately aware of their own rights in a just universe. Grassroots religion, which allows the individual to be somewhat revelatory by himself, without the backing of an institution, is growing as an alternative to churches; there is more hunger for personal religious experience, as opposed to traditions that dwell on old legends and stories of past saints and spiritual heroes.

Furthermore, political changes are bringing more countries into large political associations, such as the United Nations, in which nationalism gives ground to a larger fraternity of nations, sometimes arousing fear that one's country will lose some of its sovereignty. Eventually, all nations may be able to share intelligence and free access with all others. Churches, and even whole religions, will share insights and no longer fend each other off. A world community is becoming more possible, beginning already with worldwide communications.

Nevertheless, astrology may now be the Achilles' heel of Nostradamus' method. The art of astrological interpretation is changing, shifting its ground, and it may be moving right out from under Nostradamus' method. Since the growth of modern depth psychology, especially in the twentieth century, astrology has divided into two major streams, with the newer stream now coloring most modern work. In Nostradamus' time, astrology was what is now called "traditional astrology," a type that is still evident in many books and in much professional practice, but fading; and as it fades, it disperses the old gloom that it had for centuries cast over human prospects. The newer astrology uses all of the old chart elements, proceeds as astrology normally did, but it sees the various planets, the angles between them ("aspects") and "houses" in the light of depth psychology and a more spiritual view of one's freedom and possibilities. One way to put this is that astrology is moving into the Aquarian Age it predicted, along with everything else in our culture. It therefore is not remaining the same measuring rod that Nostradamus used. That can raise questions about the validity of his use of it, or rather, about the applicability of predictions he made with a Piscean astrology about a time when Aquarian astrology would be most accurate.

Astrology has been under fire for being occult, a brother of other, more clearly illusory, practices that were prescientific superstitions. In Nostradamus' day, this was taken for granted, for the supernatural was considered a reliable source of real information. For example, if a person wanted to know about cosmology or whether there was any life elsewhere in the universe, he or she consulted the Bible. Science had not yet freed itself from the Church. But regardless of whether one sympathizes with it, astrology is now not occult. It is a system of astronomical calculations overlaid by a highly symbolic relationship between nature and the psyche. It tries to do something that is not yet given much credit in the natural sciences—it tries to coordinate the movements of the earth and the solar system with psychology. Astrological interpretations may then be advanced without disputing any known facts about the planets. This is a remarkable change with important implications for Nostradamus' work.

Modern astrological theory has discarded, among other things, an old and crippling cosmology that regarded planets as somewhat mystical entities, able to radiate energies that influenced people's lives and determined their character and destinies. Some ideas about the planets even made them supernatural powers of a sort, and places to which the soul might even go after death. A clash of paradigms is taking place, and Nostradamus' work with astrology is located somewhere in the drama, not actually doing as well as he might have hoped. How differently did he see the old art as contrasted to its modern counterpart?

A birthchart is basically a picture of the sky both above and below the Earth as it would appear to an all-seeing eye at the time and place of one's birth. The heavens are now thought to reflect character, enabling the astrologer to read the sky, especially the planets, as a set of symbols of how the elements of character were organized when one was born. The result will shift depending on the place of birth. To read it for anything more than fundamental character and inclinations and go into the future is thought by more astrologers than ever before to drift into fortune telling.

Through the psychology of Carl Jung, and further development mainly by the philosopher Dane Rudhyar, astrology has been re-explained as an example of syncronicity, not planetary forces.

As Jung explained, every moment has its own character, and anything that begins in that moment shares the character of that moment. He pointed out that syncronicity is an "acausal connecting principle," meaning that two simultaneous and related events can occur without a detectable cause connecting one with the other. It is also often referred to as "meaningful coincidence." Furthermore, one event is internal and the other is material or external, and each will seem to symbolize the other. This gave him a basis for asserting a connection between the inner world and the outer one. He asserted that whatever is born in the moment partakes of the character of that moment, though the character of that moment has to be translated from somewhat symbolic appearances.

The symbolism, startlingly enough, directly copies the symbolism of the more subterranean levels of the mind. That is, one has to read the character of the outside event using the symbolic language of the unconscious mind, a stable reality in psychoanalysis, the interpretation of dreams, and so on, that had been previously studied by psychologists.

What this idea does is to remind us of a fairly constant teaching in esoteric disciplines: spirit and nature correspond to each other. If something very important to spirit must happen, something outside that symbolizes or suggests it may happen also. The one alerts us to the other and confirms it. You can see reality from the outside, or you can see it from the inside. On the outside, the solar system at some moment takes on a particular look, and on the inside any living thing or process born in that moment takes on the corresponding character. The trick lies in how you read the external cues and appearances so that you can link the one with the other. Astrology is essentially just such a system of links, little more.

An alternative to syncronicity is that two (or more) effects may be caused by a another thing that is out of view. It remains possible for the effects to be confused with a cause and its effect until the cause of both has been found. In this case, of course, the supposed cause was the planets, until it was agreed that the planets can't really be a cause of character. Then one may look for something else that causes character *and* planetary motions, or which just runs the universe in general. Astrology can be seen as merely a way of systematically inferring the presence of certain aspects of character from the presence of certain planetary motions and positions. That is, it merely notices that A occurs with B, it doesn't say that A is responsible for B.

Syncronicity is now the top theory, and it has given birth to a more psychologically oriented astrology. Jung used astrology in his sessions with a patient as a source of insight into the kind of person he was actually dealing with. The information could then affect his analysis of a current problem, telling him more about the larger psychological structure that surrounded and could comment on it.

On the other hand, traditional astrology, as used by Nostradamus, was much more event-centered, and it therefore tended to be concerned more with material reality than is modern astrology. Traditional astrology encouraged fatalism because it predicted the unfolding of events that were supposedly written in the stars.

Some awkward vestiges of the old astrology still appear in the literature and in readings. For example, weird things may happen to those born under the sign of Scorpio because of the sign's ungoverned depths that could harbor all sorts of supernatural forces and obsessions. Sex and death are morosely dealt with. Scorpio and the related eighth house also have much to do with other people's money. Books are still published that dwell obsessively on bequests, insurance, taxes, and inheritances, whenever Scorpio and the eighth house are involved.

What the new view amounts to is that the universe is symbolic. Slice the local solar system any particular way, and you come up with symbolic information about the quality of our particular moments, some reflection of character or psychological meaning down here. The solar system is one huge syncronicity in motion, precisely marching through its cycles, an unending string of evolving moments, changes in personality or spirit that may take outward form in storms, babies, anything that emerges out of the moment and becomes a frozen record of it. The idea ties in with general trends in mysticism and esoteric disciplines, including concepts of correspondence between spirit and nature, the inner world and the outer one.

The new psychological emphasis made astrology define inner states, not outer ones. Both Jung and Rudhyar then built it as a new approach to depth psychology. What came out of Rudhyar's work was what he called Humanistic Astrology, a system that avoids most of the classic misgivings.

One of the characteristics of this new psychological approach is that it does not forecast bad people, or even good ones. No one has a bad chart or a good chart, only a set of opportunities that will need to be understood, just as a new car requires a driver who has some training and education in the proper use of its features. The chart presents only tendencies to show a life or inner structure of a certain morally neutral type. What one then does with it is not ordained by astrology but by one's freedom of choice. People are good or bad, not their charts.

The old lines of tension between planets in a chart become not "bad aspects"—curses or liabilities, as in Nostradamus' time—but challenges to push through to a particular set of broad new powers and abilities that so far have been very difficult to handle. They promise growth, more comprehensive powers, and strength of character if one could see their potentials, and they would grant a stronger will.

Similarly, the "good aspects," lines of easy action, are not necessarily money in the bank—the "easy" aspect can encourage laziness. The "malefic" planets, such as restrictive Saturn and violent Mars, are recast, contrary to Nostradamus' era, as maturity, wisdom, and determination to see things through, if one wants that to be the case. Mars, the god of war in mythology, was, in charts that featured a strong Mars, basically a reservoir of aggressive energy looking for a sense of direction, not a predisposition to run over people or issues or join the military. The responsibility one took on in life was therefore to grow and integrate, shepherd all of these forces so that a truly impressive individual could be the result.

This kind of astrology would not be able to yield predictions of any particular kind unless people let their lives, their "givens," run off with them without trying to grow. But in Nostradamus' day there was less in astrology that could be affected by human choices, and therefore more that could be written in the stars as fate. Was he relying too much on an astrology that had not yet fully recognized how much people can change? If so, would he have been able to accurately predict the future? The future is predictable if our lives are governed by various fates. But if not, then the future becomes indeterminate. For Nostradamus' followers, these are now important questions.

According to the modern view, a chart should tell us of inner conflicts first, psychological realities, and leave the physical outcomes to more remote possibilities. Disasters and outbreaks of war belong to the most external and lowest levels of fulfillment, reachable only if inner creativity should absolutely fail. Just how much one can expect physical upheaval and riots in the streets from a chart that only maps the character of the choices people must face is very questionable. Deep conflicts in the character of a city or a nation, as presented by the chart cast for its birth, could merely represent the character of its debates in otherwise peaceful neighborhoods. Or there could be serious rumblings in the media, followed by governmental concern. How one handles conflict in a chart now depends on too many factors for it to convert easily into an apocalyptic scene.

Jean-Charles de Fontbrune, a scholar of Nostradamus' work who carried on his father's attempts to penetrate the mystery of this fascinating man, wrote:

> History, and events that lie ahead, almost always completely contradict in both matter and manner the times which we are living through. This is why so few can aspire to the perception the prophet has tried to transmit to posterity. The obstacle to understanding the spirit of prophecy lies basically in the antagonism between vision and rationalism. Adherents of the latter cannot abandon their system of logic to enter into any other form of reasoning. The essential requirement for getting to grips with prophecy is a very open mind.[7]

Even a scholar of Nostradamus's work and a supporter of his "cause" offers a broad hint that we may need to look for higher and less conventional meanings than we normally would.

So far, what recommends Nostradamus to the modern man or woman seems to be his powerful imagery. That makes him the marketing expert's dream for a high-ratings television program on the millennium. He is a superstar, especially for the media, who have starred him in shows of sepulchral mystery and special effects. We can imagine a meeting high up in television network offices: someone says, "Want to beat out the other networks? Let's bring in Nostradamus with truckloads of color—people love that stuff." They do. It's great for a night with warm company and gallons of popcorn.

[7]Fontbrune, xxviii–xxix.

CHAPTER V

EDGAR CAYCE

Christ will sit with the American delegation at Versailles. If the purpose for which its leader has gone there is accomplished, the world will experience a millennium.[1]

We now move from a very literal and external concept of the millennium to a more internal one, a millennium of the mind and heart. This is the new concept of such a great turning point. In this chapter, we look at such a personal millennium, how one remarkable man in recent history turned a corner in his life, mastering unique challenges to enlarge his life and his consciousness of higher powers. In the next chapters, we find this kind of new and previously hidden millennium finally brought into the light as a new view of people, history, and the Scriptures that had actually begun centuries ago.

Edgar Cayce was born on a farm in Hopkinsville, Kentucky, on March 18, 1877. He completed only the ninth

[1] A reading by Edgar Cayce in 1917, found in Thomas Sugrue, *There is a River: The Story of Edgar Cayce* (New York: Henry Holt & Co., Inc., 1942), 302.

grade. After his school years, Cayce didn't read much; when he did read, he preferred fiction and popular books. According to his own account, he regarded himself as the "dumbest man in Christian County" when he was awake. But when he was asleep—well, under hypnosis he had an amazing ability to give accurate, effective medical diagnoses and advice. He was sought out to give "readings" that diagnosed medical conditions and prescribed remedies.

Cayce's readings were expressed in complex medical terminology that dumbfounded him when he read the notes they produced, for he had no medical books or apparatus in his small house. Furthermore, his readings were spoken in a rather convoluted syntax, hard to interpret in places—very unlike his own personable and down-home style—with a machine-like use of impersonal terms and references. "This body" was the subject, and the person who requested the reading was referred to as "this entity." The analyses were devastatingly accurate but put across with anything but a good bedside manner. One can easily imagine the information coming out in a metallic voice.

Cayce gave only two readings a day. Any more left him feeling tired. He was not conscious of what he was telling people, and he didn't even know what the conductor, the person posing the questions, was asking. He was totally unable to keep track of events once he was unconscious. Later in his fascinating psychic career, the possibility of subterfuge by the conductor would become a contentious issue.

The scenario for a typical reading was that a stenographer would take down Cayce's statements and give a copy to the patient. An assistant, usually a medical doctor or a trained hypnotist, would then add whatever he thought was necessary. Interestingly enough, although Cayce was successful at giving these readings, he maintained his livelihood by working as a professional photographer.

Edgar's grandfather had been a successful water witcher. He too had experienced some strange things. He had seen some normally invisible things, and he could make objects move without touching them; for example, he could make brooms dance. There was no other history of psychic powers in the family, with the possible exception of Edgar's father, Leslie B. Cayce, who found that snakes liked him; unfortunately, Leslie hated them. Nevertheless, they would follow him home, sometimes winding themselves around his hat brim if he put it on the ground. That disturbed Leslie so much that he gave up farming.

As a child, Edgar did not seem to adjust well to the world around him. He seemed abstracted, unable to concentrate on ordinary studies, and he had unusual experiences that at the time could only be dismissed with skepticism. He played with friends, other little boys and girls, whom no one could see, except occasionally his mother. As he grew up, these imaginary playmates did also. When he tried to point them out to someone, they would disappear. They did not want to be seen by anyone else. Sometimes he could also see his deceased grandfather puttering around in the barn. When he looked hard at any of these people, he noticed that he could see right through them.

By the time he was twelve years old, Edgar was a very devoted young Christian who resolved to read the entire Bible every year of his life. He had built a little playhouse for himself in the woods near a creek on the Cayce property. He went there to read from his Bible one day when he looked up and saw a woman standing before him. He did not recognize her, but he noticed what looked like wings partly visible behind her back. She said to him, "Your prayers have been answered, little boy. Tell me what it is you want most of all, so that I may give it to you." Although very frightened, he replied that he wanted to be helpful to other people, especially children. Then the woman disappeared.

The angelic lady appeared once again and told him that, if he would sleep with his head on his schoolbooks, she could help him with his studies. The next day in school, he was asked to spell a list of words and couldn't do it. That night he slept on the book; later, in school he was able to spell all of the words. He continued to sleep on his books and found that he knew his lessons, even the entire contents of a book, when he woke up. His teachers would ask him about an item, and he would see the page that contained the information in his mind and literally read the image as if the book were open in front of him. Apparently, he did not necessarily *learn* his lessons in this unusual way. The clear, readable image suggests clairvoyance. He was not actually remembering his answers, but was reading the answer.

The first instance in which Cayce publicly displayed his psychic gift occurred when he was a grown man. He had contracted a hoarseness of voice that would not clear up. At the time, hypnotism was very popular as an adjunct to medicine. A traveling hypnotist was giving demonstrations of its power in Hopkinsville. He became interested in Cayce's condition and tried to cure him. With the town following the story in the local newspaper, the *Hopkinsville New Era*, the hypnotist put Cayce under. His voice cleared up, but when he came out of trance, it was suddenly hoarse again. Other hypnotists tried, but none could solve the problem—Cayce for some reason would not accept "post-suggestion," the ability to enter or maintain a suggested state after reviving. He apparently was taking over in "stage three," the deepest hypnotic state, when post-suggestions could be accepted.

One of the hypnotists who had worked on Cayce suggested that, during this third stage, Cayce be asked to comment on his own condition, a treatment that had worked in some cases before. In Hopkinsville, there was only one hypnotist, Al C. Layne. On March 31, 1901, Layne had Cayce go under one more time. Cayce, who was becoming impatient with these sessions, had resolved that if this strategy didn't work, he would accept no more hypnotic treatments. He hadn't been eating or sleeping, and his health was deteriorating. Layne asked the unconscious Cayce to comment on his own condition and speak in a normal tone of voice. What happened next was astonishing.

After a few minutes, Cayce began to mumble, then he cleared his throat and said,

Yes, we can see the body. In the normal state, this body is unable to speak, due to a partial paralysis of the inferior muscles of the vocal cords, produced by nerve strain. This is a psychological condition producing a physical effect. This may be removed by increasing the circulation to the affected parts by suggestion while in this unconscious condition.[2]

Layne told the "body" to increase circulation in the affected parts. Cayce's upper chest and throat became pink, then red. After twenty minutes, he said, "It is all right now." Layne was told to suggest that the condition return to normal, and the body awaken. The patient woke up and spoke in a clear voice.

Jubilation erupted in the room, and soon Cayce and the others were contemplating a new healing technique that could have widespread use. It was the beginning of his career as a clairvoyant healer.

No one really knew how this process worked; Cayce was as amazed and mystified as everyone else. As has been mentioned, it is in fact rare that a psychic knows much more than that he or she can perform, and an analytical approach to these states, trying to understand them as would an observing psychologist, is apparently difficult to maintain. How psychic states work is evidently a mystery that people other than the psychic must penetrate.

Layne himself had been beset with stomach problems that wouldn't go away. He had been to various doctors, but none had been able to cure him. Finally, he brought over a list of questions for Cayce, who put himself to sleep; Layne then asked for advice. He got it—a list of his symptoms and a regimen of therapy, complete with recommended diet,

[2]Sugrue, 107.

medicines, and exercises. When Cayce woke up and read the list Layne had scribbled down, he found that it had medical terms and names of medicines that were completely unknown to him.

The operative word so far to describe Edgar Cayce's abilities had been *clairvoyance.* Cayce was, and still is, considered a clairvoyant. Clairvoyance, the ability to see things normally hidden or at a distance, applied to his ability to see what was inside of books even without opening and reading them, but it actually had only limited application to his readings of medical problems. The information and judgment required of good medical diagnosis can hardly be attributed to mere clairvoyance. The information was also delivered in the stilted style typical of medical journals, a type of literature that Cayce never read. Furthermore, the voice referred to itself as *we*, not *I.*

One possible explanation was proposed by Cayce's mother: we all have a kind of universal knowledge or awareness inside of ourselves, although we are not consciously aware of it. However, if Cayce were merely opening up a secret cache of knowledge that we all have encoded in our deeper recesses, then why did this inner knowledge also have a different temperament and personality from his waking personality? This inner self also had different skills, such as the ability to make medical judgments that requires training and experience that the conscious man did not possess. As the description of this inner self progresses, it begins to look more and more like another person, not Cayce himself. At this point, we enter deep inside the world of the paranormal, the possibility that Cayce's observations were actually made by other personalities working through his mind. This hardly fits the categories of a personal "depth psychology," though depth psychology has strained to contain and explain the paranormal.

Cayce's other experiences suggest that there is another realm altogether, such as the one that constantly illuminated his childhood. His problems as an adult with intrusive powers and their natural obligations batted him like a tennis ball between his desire to let go to other dimensions of reality that he genuinely knew about and pressures to stay in the conventional world, learn his lessons, and make a living.

Besides the evidence of other personalities, there is a naturalistic fallacy in ordinary thinking. At the cost of excluding very suggestive experiences, we usually accept that minds are located in ordinary space and time. I am here, you are there, and the distance between us is just the number of miles or feet between your body and mine. But that leads to the conclusion that mind is just what can be so located—the central nervous system, which is purely material, although highly complex. Destroy it, and the person must cease to exist. The paranormal, on the other hand, suggests that mind is only somewhat contained in, and is not identical with, any material complexity. What it may do or achieve on its own, independently of its container, is then an open question. Other minds could very well get into the act.

Layne's stomach condition improved remarkably. He and Cayce set up an office in Hopkinsville and began to practice "suggestive therapeutics and osteopathy." Cayce, however, was not enthusiastic about this step. He was afraid that, if his advice were wrong, he could kill somebody. Layne assured him that, as a hypnotist, he himself knew enough about medicine to detect any dangerous remedies. Moreover, if a diagnosis required potentially dangerous prescription drugs, he wouldn't be able to get them since he wasn't a medical doctor. He would ask Cayce, or his higher self, about an available substitute.

Cayce wanted his patients' identities to remain strictly anonymous. He didn't want to know anything about them, before or after he was in trance. He was not even to see them; they would wait outside his reading room for their advice. He refused to take any money. His successes flowed steadily; but for some mysterious reason he did need to know *where* the patient was located, outside of his office. Yet, despite the fact that his clients either improved or were cured, Cayce operated under constant fear, feeling that he needed to kill only one person to be a murderer. Because of this fear, only a few knew that he was giving out diagnoses and remedies. As far as the world at large was aware, he was a photographer.

When Layne decided to go to school and get professional training, Cayce began to work with three other doctors, but chiefly with Dr. John Blackburn. He would need several consulting doctors because it was evident from his readings that he was a man without any medical prejudices who would advise across the whole spectrum of medical practice and philosophy, including the highly unorthodox. For example, he once told a woman that she had a laceration of the stomach; her doctors should be ignored. Instead, she should take a lemon every morning, roll it, cut it in half, and eat one of the halves. She should then walk as far as she could, stop and rest, walk back home, sprinkle salt on the other half, eat it, and immediately drink two glasses of water. In a few weeks after following this strange routine, she felt much better.

Nevertheless, Cayce's misgivings about his work continued. He realized that he didn't believe in himself or his apparent mission. He also had to endure the insults of an earlier rebellion against his kind of work, which had been given the pejorative label *somnambulism*. In the wake of experiments with the relatively new practice of hypnosis, it had been noticed that on occasion someone in trance would diagnose the medical condition of the person next to him, or even that of someone at a distance. These diagnoses were disturbingly accurate, but conventional medicine rebelled when somnambulism threatened to become a movement in Europe. A surge of adamant skepticism worked, and by Cayce's time conventional medicine was back in command. But he had to contend with its sometimes destructive doubt and on one occasion even had to suffer at its hands.

One day, while he was lying in trance, demonstrating his abilities, some doctors who had not seen him work before got into an argument about what kind of conscious or unconscious state he was in. Over Dr. Blackburn's vehement protests, one then stuck a needle in Cayce's arms, hands, and feet. Cayce didn't respond. Another found a hatpin and thrust it clear through the unconscious man's cheek. Still no response. A third doctor then took a penknife, inserted it under the nail of Cayce's little finger and lifted the fingernail slowly away. No blood appeared, and he still lay quietly.

Suddenly Cayce awoke and felt the pain. The doctors quickly explained that they had been conducting a few scientific experiments, but he exploded in righteous anger. He denounced them and said, "I'm through. No matter how many miracles you see, you will never believe anything that will interfere with your smugness. You take it for granted that every man in the world is crooked except yourselves. And you will accept no proof of anyone's honesty. . . . I'll never give another reading unless it's for someone who needs help and believes I can give it to him."[3] Then he walked out. The fingernail never did grow back normally.

Cayce eventually got a job as a photographer in Alabama, waiting to establish himself before calling his wife Gertrude to come and join him. Meanwhile, back in Hopkinsville, Dr. Wesley H. Ketchum, a close friend and associate for whom Cayce had performed a reading, began to contact other doctors, as well as psychologists in the United States and Europe, to tell them of Cayce's powers. From the look of the various newspaper clippings Cayce received, interest was spreading like a prairie fire. Ketchum had a movement going, and he wanted Cayce to join him, along with Albert D. Noe who owned the Latham Hotel in Hopkinsville, and "the squire"— Edgar's father—to establish an office that would offer Cayce's readings.

Cayce now had to confront his soul, for the entire matter was becoming very serious. Should he consider himself called to a special mission? As always, he was reluctant, unable to give up old hopes of a normal life. But Ketchum was clearly good at organizing things, and he was shining a brilliant spotlight on Cayce.

---

[3] Sugrue, 138.

Cayce sat up all night in his Alabama studio and prayed. Near morning, he finally opened his Bible and in the dark pointed to a place on a page. Then he waited for the sun to come up so that he could see what he was pointing at. It was Psalm 46:

God is our refuge and our strength, a very present help in trouble.

Therefore will we not fear, though the earth be removed, and though the mountains be carried into the midst of the sea;

Though the waters thereof roar and be troubled, though the mountains shake with the swelling thereof. Selah.

There is a river, the streams whereof will make glad the city of God.

Cayce then wrote a letter to Ketchum setting out his conditions. Among others, he demanded that his readings were not to be considered his livelihood. For that, he would need a complete photographic studio. In addition, he stipulated that only sick people who made a request on their own would get readings. Stenographic records of all readings would be kept, one copy for the patient and one for the files. He would give no more than two readings a day because he had discovered that he was inwardly exhausted after only two.

Cayce still had to understand himself. He had no idea how his readings worked. He would read over the record of a session and be completely confused about what was coming out of him. He had no idea what the medical terms meant. He could guide himself to sleep for rest or for a reading, as if he had two kinds of sleep to choose from, but he had no sense of doing anything afterwards.

Dr. Ketchum reported the Cayce phenomenon to the American Society of Clinical Research in Boston, and it was reported in the *New York Times* of October 9, 1910:

Edgar Cayce's mind is amenable to suggestion, the same as all other subconscious minds, but in addition thereto it has the power to interpret to the objective mind of others what it acquired from the subconscious state of other individuals of the same kind. The subconscious mind forgets nothing. The conscious mind receives the impression from without and transfers all thought to the subconscious, where it remains even though the conscious be destroyed.

The term *subconscious mind* was used in the popular literature of the time, and even today, as a catchall word for anything evidently going on in the mind that we do not keep track of and may find surprising. The conscious mind cannot keep track of everything in the brain, at least because the brain cannot think and contemplate its thinking at the same time—much necessarily must remain "unconscious." The effort would be equivalent to turning the eye around so that it might see the optic nerve and pick out the operations that make the eye work.

In other systems, however, other terms are used. In Jungian psychology, the subconscious is likely to be the *collective unconscious*, or the less deeply secluded *personal unconscious*. Not that these things are actually unconscious; they are not available to the conscious mind under normal conditions. The many tiers of the mind are not easy to understand, but they do betray their presence. Without them, the conscious self could not operate.

In Emanuel Swedenborg's psychology, which we will discuss in the next chapters, the unity of the mind with other minds at these higher levels prompts the term *spiritual world*. The spiritual world is not another space/time alongside the physical universe so much as it is the realm of mind itself. It is not even a *realm* so much as one Mind in which everyone participates and which has a divine core. Thus, we live in Mind, and it seems to be a solid world to us, but its relative inertness in the "natural" state inspires us to regard it as merely material, for it does not display all of its responsiveness to our thoughts and feelings at this level. Like the rind of a fruit, this outer side of Mind remains deceptively stable and unreactive, like a person whose mind is made up. Things are likely to stay where they are unless moved. The possibilities for future developments in the leading theories of physics are vast, however, and Edgar Cayce's experiences only hinted at them.

Meanwhile, Gertrude gave birth to their second son, Milton Porter. To their horror the baby got sick, worsened, and died. This was astonishing: though there had been plenty of time for it, no readings were done for the infant. Edgar came to realize too late that he still didn't believe in providing for himself or his own interests as he had responded to the faith and needs of others. *They* believed in him, and that had inspired him to respond to *them*. He had never decided whether he believed in the readings himself. This hole in his ethical consciousness had all along been quietly neglected, left unnoticed, until little Milton was lost. After this tragic episode, Cayce applied his gifts to his family when needed. And his intervention was needed soon afterward when Gertrude became ill. After an unorthodox therapy that included heroin and fumes from apple brandy, she recovered.

On the business end, the team discovered that it was one thing to give readings and another to get the diagnoses and remedies carried out if the team needed medical assistance. Many doctors disbelieved Cayce's readings and would revert to their own diagnoses or refuse the case altogether. Because of this problem, the partners decided that a hospital specifically dedicated to following the readings was needed, and specialists in the many fields mentioned in his readings had to be brought in. But it would be a very expensive project.

Unfortunately, no one who had such vast amounts of money was offering it. The scientists were turning away, and the rich would promise but never contribute. The money coming in was volunteered, and it amounted to very small amounts per person, when it was there at all. The medical world's widespread resistance to administering Cayce's cures down to the last detail meant that proof of his method couldn't be obtained. The cures would remain unrecognized because seldom or never actually tried. The little company was going nowhere.

As these money troubles were accumulating, Cayce discovered that a patient who had written to him requesting treatment—one of his stipulations for entering into the company—had not been answered. He also noticed that he had been experiencing headaches after his readings, which he had not previously. He asked Ketchum, who had been acting as his conductor, to explain. Ketchum admitted that, while Cayce was unconscious, he had not been asking for the kind of readings Cayce had thought he was; Edgar could not actually tell in his "sleep" what kind of information was being requested. Rather than strictly medical and humanitarian readings, other readings were requested concerning monetary income, including gambling. Ketchum clearly hoped that Cayce would sympathize; he told Cayce that this information was kept from him so that he wouldn't worry.

Cayce just got up and walked out. He announced to his wife that he was leaving Ketchum and Noe. She was very happy about it. Not too much later they moved to Selma, Alabama, where Cayce became much happier as a photographer who did only occasional readings, usually for friends. One large source of younger friends was his popular Sunday School and Bible classes. When the young men in these classes went to war in Europe in 1917, they wrote that his lessons helped them retain their sanity and faith under hellish conditions. Despite the dissolution of his partnership with Ketchum and Noe, the thought that a hospital had to be built to carry out Cayce's treatments was not forgotten. Unfortunately, it would be seventeen years after Ketchum and Noe left the scene before the hospital would be a reality.

One of Cayce's readings had indicated that he would not succeed in getting a hospital built until he could include a person of the Jewish faith in his plans. David Kahn, a dedicated young Jew, had come into Cayce's life after Edgar had done a reading for the Kahn family. David became a staunch and very optimistic friend, determined to make the hospital real.

Another important Jewish friend was Morton Harry Blumenthal, a stockbroker in New York, who contributed the money to establish the hospital in Virginia Beach, Virginia.

In his readings, Cayce had been told that Virginia Beach should be the site of his clinic because he should live near a large body of water. Water was good for his health and for psychic sensitivity. Furthermore, people who would come to the readings should approach over water. It would put them in the right "vibration" and state of mind for the readings. Their state of mind or attitude was in fact important to the success of the readings. Virginia Beach was also an overnight trip from New York, Philadelphia, Baltimore, and Washington. It would be far enough away to allow people to put their mundane lives behind them, but near enough to interest them in coming. Nearby Tidewater also had a busy and prosperous future.

In the meantime, readings on metaphysics and theology had begun. The new center would not only be medically effective, but it would try to deal with problems of consciousness and outlook. Shortly before Blumenthal showed up, a man named Arthur Lammers had walked briskly into Cayce's life and overwhelmed him with suggestions that he use his powers to get insights into philosophical and metaphysical questions, enlarge the mind as well as heal the body.

Cayce liked the idea, but he felt that Lammers' ideas were strange. Cayce's spirituality was formed from the Bible and Christian preaching; Lammers was filled with zeal for the "ancient mysteries," expounding passionately on astrology, reincarnation, the wisdom of Egypt, and other things that, he claimed, predated and explained Christian teachings. Cayce pleaded ignorance of anything on such an esoteric scale; but he was interested, and he found that his readings, once consulted, did come up with ideas that were analogous to ancient teachings. Reincarnation was attractive to people as a general explanation of what is more academically described as the "unconscious" givens that we have to deal with. Cayce would later feature one's past lives as an optional "Life Reading"; everyone had one or more past lives, the readings said, for no new souls had been created since the beginning. Evidently, once the door was open to other "subconscious" minds, one could walk through to any school of thought he might be interested in.

Since the duplicity of Ketchum and Noe, Gertrude was now the conductor for all of her husband's readings. One further condition affecting the readings was that the person for whom they were given needed to have faith. The conductor was uniquely important; he or she was the link between Cayce and his normal life, and a good link with normal energies during the readings was evidently psychically necessary for Cayce's wellbeing. When Gertrude was the conductor, the readings went well.

On May 6, 1927, the Association of National Investigators was incorporated in the state of Virginia. It would later become the Association of Research and Enlightenment (ARE). Its stated purpose was "to engage in general psychic research, and to provide for the practical application of any knowledge obtainable through the medium of psychic phenomena." Blumenthal was president; Hugh Lynn, who was Cayce's son, and David Kahn were among the vice-presidents; Cayce himself was secretary and treasurer; and Gertrude was on the board of trustees. Anyone asking for a reading had first to join the association, agreeing that he or she was participating in an experiment in psychic research. This was a legal protection. Members would have access to the facilities, including the hospital and all data, though the names of people who owned the readings might be withheld.

One day Dr. William Moseley Brown, head of the Psychology Department at Washington and Lee University, boasted to his class that he could expose any psychic. Hugh Lynn was a student in his class, and he challenged Brown to expose his father. Brown went to the association and met the elder Cayce, telling him of his challenge and of Hugh Lynn's response. The two men shook hands and sat down to talk and to review readings. Brown said, "I can't expose it. Still, it's not the sort of thing you can do nothing about. I can't ignore it. I'll have to believe in it." He joined the association and got a reading of his own, and some for members of his family. Edgar was moved. "The millennium has come," he said.

Edgar Cayce had experienced his own, inner millennium. But he would later make statements about the one he believed was waiting for everyone outside.

Cayce's statements about the millennium appear grounded in the imagery that is commonly found in millennial movements (indeed, in his youth, Cayce met the Fundamentalist evangelist Dwight L. Moody and discussed the Bible with him.) His millennial visions describe physical changes, such as the reshaping of continents, the eruption of volcanoes, the upheaval of earthquakes. New land masses will be seen in the Atlantic and Pacific Oceans. Parts of New York will disappear, but Virginia Beach—the locale of "the entity"—will luckily remain safe. In reading 397-15, given on Jan. 19, 1934, Cayce indicates that these troubles "will begin in those periods in '58 to '98" when "His light will be seen again in the clouds."

In one reading, no. 826-8, given on August 11, 1936, Cayce is asked, "What great change or the beginning of what change, if any, is to take place in the earth in the year 2000 to 2001 A.D.?" The "entity" responds enigmatically, "When there is the shifting of the poles, or a new cycle begins."

All this turmoil culminates in the Second Coming of Christ, which will be accomplished, according to Cayce's reading no. 5749-4 of June 28, 1932, "when those who are His have made the way clear, passable, for Him to come." Cayce also indicates that Christ will appear in the same body that he occupied while he lived on earth. Furthermore, in reading 5749-7, he adds:

> He will come again and receive His own, those who have prepared themselves through belief in Him and acting in that manner; for the Spirit is abroad, and the time draws near, and there will be the reckoning. . . . And art THOU ready to give account of what thou hast done with thine opportunity in the earth as the Sons of God, as the heirs and joint heirs of glory with the Son? Then make thy paths straight, for there must come an answering for what thou hast done

with thy Lord! He will not tarry; for having overcome, He will appear even as the Lord and Master. . . . [T]hose who are faithful and just in their reckoning shall be caught up with Him to rule and to do judgment for a thousand years.

Notice that these readings present original information about future changes on the planet, but questions about the Second Coming are referred back to the Bible. Essentially, the message is to stick with normal studies of Scripture. Nothing is said that isn't included in the Last Judgment teachings in the Gospels or Revelation. People must live good lives in obedience to the Lord. This was a theme in Cayce's other prophecies about the last times, as well. If people improve their lives, the last days of the era will go well.

What is not so clear is the condition of the planet. This kind of material upheaval is common in millenarian prophecies. They are almost totally depressing—so much so that they call attention to themselves as a distinct phenomenon requiring special analysis.

Why should Earth go through so much upheaval that all life is threatened? And why do psychics routinely come up with statements about physical disaster? Be that as it may, can the *spiritual* future be better, or will it be worse?

Part Two

A NEW AGE

CHAPTER VI

EMANUEL SWEDENBORG

Science, Emanuel Swedenborg said, trains the mind to be intelligent so that it may finally perceive an orderly spiritual reality. Rarely do we find someone in the pursuit of spiritual wisdom who enjoyed such intriguing access to it and reinforced his ideas with so much systematic thinking as did Swedenborg. His detailed and organized understanding of spiritual experience presents a method through which old puzzles and trends in millenarian prophecies may finally be understood.

Swedenborg began his career as a scientist and technologist. His accomplishments in those two fields are almost too many to mention in any non-encyclopedic work. He was a very independent thinker who would, even in his more mature years, enter a field, master it, and push out its frontiers. A scientific study at Stanford University of the probable IQs of historical figures, based on an adaptation of the Stanford-Binet intelligence test, rated his IQ at somewhere beyond 200, the limit of the test. He was accompanied up there only by Johann Wolfgang von Goethe and John Stuart Mill.

Swedenborg immersed himself in astronomy, mechanics, chemistry, scientific philosophy, mineralogy, psychology, and physiology, setting new precedents in all of them and anticipating a number of later discoveries and inventions. His scientific and technological interests absorbed him almost completely until he reached his mid-fifties, when his life was changed by an astonishing introduction to a new level of thought and experience.

Emanuel Swedenborg was born in Stockholm, Sweden, in 1688, the third child of a Lutheran regimental chaplain, Jesper Swedberg.[1] When he was fifteen, his father was appointed bishop of Skara. As one would expect, he grew up with a strong, basic Christian faith. While a boy, he surprised people with his spiritual insights, and he practiced a meditation technique, based on the control of his breath, a yogic method, which was largely unknown outside of Eastern religions. He wasn't interested in studying theology, though; instead, he confessed an "immoderate love" for science and technology.[2]

When he was twenty-two, and just emerging from Uppsala University, this immoderate love drove him to England to converse with Isaac Newton and other scientists. He didn't succeed in meeting Newton, but he did spend time with two prominent men of science—the first Astronomer Royal of England, John Flamsteed, and Edmund Halley, for whom Halley's comet is named.

Swedenborg was determined to help Sweden become competitive with other European countries in science and technology. The great era of astronomical discovery had just ended. Commerce by sea needed efficient solutions to navigational problems, and "positional" astronomy took center stage. Swedenborg threw himself into the complicated mathematics of positional astronomy and quickly found a solution to the very difficult problem of how to find the longitude at sea. It

[1]The family was ennobled by Queen Ulrika Eleonora in 1719, hence the name "Swedenborg."

[2]Cyriel O. Sigstedt, The Swedenborg Epic (New York: Bookman Associates, 1952), 21. This book was reprinted in 1981 by the Swedenborg Society, London.

depended on the position of the moon, but the accurate lunar tables that would make it work were not yet available and would be a long time in coming. In the meantime, he established a scientific journal called *Daedalus Hyperboreus* (The Northern Daedalus), and he proposed an advanced observatory for Sweden on Mt. Kinnekulle.

Swedenborg intended—when the time was right—to present his ideas to King Charles XII, Sweden's hero king; the two men were developing a close association, and he knew that he could get the king's sympathetic consideration. But in 1718 events took a dramatic turn. Charles got involved in war against both Norway and Denmark. He wanted to lay siege to the Norwegian fortress at Fredrikshall, very near Sweden's western border, and he asked Swedenborg to design and direct a stunning effort to bypass the Danish fleet, which was patrolling the sea south of the fortress. Rather than try to sail past the Danes, Swedish warships would be transported overland to the waters of the fjord just below the fortress. The huge project was successful in spite of very severe winter weather. The fortress was almost conquered when Charles was killed in 1719. Rather than continue what was hardly a popular campaign, even for Swedenborg, the Swedes ended the seige and withdrew.

Sweden was one of the poorest countries in Europe, and it had been wasted further by the many wars of Charles XII. Mining was its most lucrative industry, and Swedenborg accepted an appointment as an extraordinary assessor (meaning something like "extra assessor") on the powerful Board of Mines. Because his family had been ennobled, he also took a seat in the Diet's House of Nobles. But as these years went by, his interests turned with more and more urgency to a classic problem, the relationship between matter and spirit.

In his *Principia*, a massive presentation of his scientific philosophy published in 1734, he expressed concern that everything in nature be explained by the creative power of the Infinite. The work traces the development of the universe from elementary particles that emerge from the Infinite and actually resemble the "virtual particles" of modern quantum physics. Through stages of increasing complexity where one form leads logically to the next by a set of simple rules, he derived all the known elements of the universe. On this purely philosophical basis, he was the first to assert that our solar system is part of a vast aggregation of stars—known to us today as the Milky Way galaxy—and that this great community is one of many others. *Principia* was also destined, much nearer our time, to arouse interest in Swedenborg as the first scientist to formulate the nebular hypothesis, a classic theory of how the solar system was formed, predating the work of both Pierre Simon de Laplace and Immanuel Kant. Swedenborg did not, however, anticipate Laplace's observations or his method. Laplace's physics are also opposite to those of Swedenborg's theory.

The *Principia* also defines the character of various elements of nature, including what was then regarded as a very mysterious force, magnetism. The work was very well received, and Swedenborg was widely recognized as one of the most learned men in Europe.

His pursuit of the link between the Infinite and the finite brought up the possibility that the seat of the soul, and therefore a substantial demonstration of the soul's existence, can be found scientifically. The presence of the soul had to have a biological basis, he felt, and he became dedicated to finding it. He was driven as always by his need to know, but he also wanted passionately to prove the existence of the soul to the educated minds all around him, very many of whom doubted any kind of spiritual reality.

At this time, during the mid-eighteenth century, established religion itself encouraged widespread skepticism about the soul when it theorized that the soul was ephemeral outside of the body, just a vapor or shapeless ghost. Many theologians theorized that we should not expect a complete world awaiting the soul after death, especially not one that looked at all familiar, like our earth. According to theologians, a full life for the soul wouldn't be available until the Last Judgment when the lonely drifting entities, the souls of the departed, would be reunited with their bodies. The bodies of the dead would be brought out of their graves and restored by a miracle, even after they had completely deteriorated.

Swedenborg was later at pains to point out that the idea of an ephemeral soul is not true to Scripture, which actually presents angels and spirits as complete people, with bodies that are spiritual, not material. They were always seen in human form. He felt that the church's thinking was due instead to a seductive naturalism that had long ago crept into Christian thought. To take the soul so closely to nonexistence could kill belief in it by making it virtually an abstraction.

Swedenborg toured European schools and institutions to master physiology and added more discoveries and creative speculations to the field; like most good science, his investigations always produced byproducts, whether or not he could solve his main problem. Then came the first sign that a great breakthrough to real knowledge of the soul might happen to him.

As he sat writing his innovative works on the soul's "kingdom," the human body, a shaft of light seemed to dart through his brain. Almost every day for several months afterwards he saw a flame; it was as vividly real as a flame in a fireplace. It seemed to tell him that his work had divine approval.

He turned his mind upward for a more intuitive way to proceed, and he soon began to have mysterious and even ominous dreams and visions that drove him into deep contemplation, especially about himself. Sensing that he was drifting into a spiritual crisis, he struggled to find out what the dreams meant. In 1744, at the age of fifty-six, his simple theology was reduced to ignorance, and his ego and intellectual pride were shown to him. He could do nothing, he felt finally, but surrender himself completely to the will of the Lord and allow himself to be instructed. As he later wrote, the Lord took him back to the Bible. He read it over many times, including the original Hebrew texts, and compiled large indexes for it. He claimed that he was also shown an inner sense in Scripture that taught about the Lord and the heavenly community. Then, in April of 1745, the spiritual world was opened to him, and he began to compose some of the most remarkable books in Christian literature on God, man, the afterlife, and the Scriptures.

Science had taught Swedenborg how to think rationally—how to handle and evaluate evidence, formulate and analyze ideas, and recognize the difference between appearances and reality. He now realized that religious thought as well should rely on these skills, even when confronted with spiritual experience. Science was, therefore, not in itself antagonistic to religion. Now he could see that the world that science studies is an expression, actually a model, of spiritual reality itself. This idea had been suggested on scattered occasions in history, but an explanation of its workings had not been formulated on any large scale, at least not since classical Greek philosophy. For him, the transition from natural science to spiritual and theological interests was not a huge break, but a natural transition to a higher level of investigation and meaningful thought.

Swedenborg did not behave like just another seer or psychic. Thousands of people have seen some part or aspect of the world of spirit, but it is difficult to find psychics or prophets who can analyze what they see and avoid further puzzles. Swedenborg's work is unique in the literature because all of his faculties were allowed to be completely intact in his experiences.[3] He was allowed to explore and study the spiritual world as if it were merely a part of his home town. He could see into it when fully awake, walking the streets, or even conversing at a party. This is critically important, for it meant that he could bring his entire mind, both his waking mind and his deeper psychic sensitivities, to the analysis of his experiences. That one simple fact allowed him to see through and reduce

---

[3]I use the term "allowed" because Swedenborg always claimed that his revelations were granted to him by a dispensation from God and were not a product of his own capacities.

their bewildering phenomena to clear conclusions, much as he had analyzed scientific evidence in laboratories or had studied critical work on dissection tables. He was, without parallel, a *spiritual scientist*.

The literature of the paranormal is voluminous, but it is characterized by excessive phenomenalism. That is, exotic experiences and phenomena proliferate and are taken at face value, and all kinds of disparate theories follow. Truly analytical thinking is rare. One reason is that psychics work in trance or under restricted conditions such as the natural limitations of dreams or visions; a seer may not even remember what he or she says in these states. Edgar Cayce actually slept, which put him at such a distance from his spiritual sources that he was for a long time unable to accept them and his status as a medium, as we have seen.

According to Swedenborg, the religious world needed this deeper, more analytical penetration of spiritual experience, for it was time for humanity to develop both a stronger awareness and a better understanding of the spiritual side of life.

The occurrence of "past-life memories" illustrates the need for deeply analytical work in the field. It sometimes happens that a person remembers things that actually never happened in this life; these "memories," therefore, suggest a past life in which these things did happen. Regressive hypnosis has been used extensively to bring out many more of these memories. Such experiences drew some comment from Swedenborg, who was, in a very real sense, on hand to examine the phenomenon from the inside:

> An angel or spirit is not permitted to speak with a man from his own memory, but only from the man's memory; for angels and spirits have a memory as well as man. If a spirit were to speak from his own memory with a man, the man would not know otherwise than that the thoughts then in his mind were his own, although they were the spirit's thoughts. This would be like the recollection of something

which the man had never heard or seen. That this is so has been given me to know from experience.

This is the source of the belief held by some of the ancients that after some thousands of years they were to return into their former life, and into everything they had done, and in fact, had returned. This they concluded because at times there came to them a sort of recollection of things that they had never seen or heard. This came from an influx from the memory of spirits into their ideas of thought.[4]

Swedenborg was able to explore the spiritual world with the necessary full consciousness for a long time—the last third of his life. His books are filled with reports, descriptions, and analyses of how the spiritual world works. Because he was able to function in both worlds, and in the other world like one of its inhabitants, angels called him "the wonderful one."

Before proceeding on to Swedenborg's reinterpretation of the Last Judgment, which follows in the next chapter, it is necessary to look at some of the implications of Swedenborg's thought and how that thought revolutionized traditional Western theology.

When a reader steps back a bit from Swedenborg's detailed discussions and ignores his traditional theological vocabulary, he or she may notice that Swedenborg's logic strongly suggests that everything, including the material world, is actually spiritual. To begin with, the whole of creation can have only one center and essence. It cannot actually be divided into two, often antagonistic, realities, for God, Swedenborg wrote, is the origin and essential reality (*esse*)

---

[4]Emanuel Swedenborg, *Heaven and Its Wonders and Hell: From Things Heard and Seen*, tr. John C. Ager, 2nd edition (West Chester, Pennsylvania: The Swedenborg Foundation, 1995), ¶ 256. Paragraph numbers are used in place of page numbers in Swedenborg studies, since they are uniform in all editions.

The possibility that *memories* can be shared in spiritual experience does not appear in the usual literature, including the literature of regressive hypnosis. But it should have been inferred from the way in which mediumship and telepathy work. Minds can and do share their contents with each other, and the fact is pervasive in literature on the paranormal.

deep inside of everything and continually maintains it as an expression of himself, all the way from heaven through the material world. The material world in Swedenborg's system is not a world off by itself which is made of a separate kind of stuff; it amounts to the spiritual world's outer and comparatively static boundary layer. There is, therefore, nothing other than spirit or heart and mind, though we have found it normally useful in theology and science to distinguish between two kinds of experiences and appearances. In the following pages, the term *mind* includes both the intellect and the heart.

What we call the natural or material world was grown just as the rind of a fruit, a naturally hard or resistant area of closure, grows from the fruit itself and then resists any further expansion of it. This rind amounts to another, rather condensed and inert, form of the fruit inside, not something basically different. Its main function is to react against the tendency of the more fluid and dynamic interior to spill out formlessly; the fruit, therefore, grows it from itself, stops potentially destructive expansion at a convenient point, holds itself in, and thereby gives itself permanence and stability.

In traditional Christian thought, nature has seemed to contradict spirit, to be even radically opposed to it. The skepticism about spirit that flows from materialistic thinking and natural instincts moved classical theologians to recommend the suppression of nature—monasteries were built, and the spirit and the flesh were thought to be in intestinal war with each other. Satan appeared to be the ruler of the world, leaving God to rule only heaven. Nature does indeed resist spirit, but in an underlying order uncomplicated by us; it does not kill spirit but only contains it. Something has to put on the brakes, for spirit is energy and creativity itself, the implacable shove forward to achieve all possible creative states and expressions. Left to itself, spirit would proliferate events and phenomena in infinite profusion and variety. Each would instantly flower and disappear so that the energy of creation could careen on to the next one. Somewhere, therefore, there has to be a source of consolidation. That source is nature.

Nature also cares for the welfare of the living offspring of spirit or mind, which can then persist and have a chance to grow and learn in an objective, stable environment. After the enormous surge of primal creativity, nature is the emergence of God's nesting instinct.

Once creation settles into somewhat predictable changes, it can also give birth to natural law and the science that studies it. The human body itself, with its spirit in some sense at home "inside," is also a model of how the universe contains spirit.

As we view either realm—the spiritual or the natural—from inside, which we always have to do, it will seem self-contained and without boundaries that would logically betray the existence of anything beyond. If the material space we know contained everything, spiritual as well as natural, then the spiritual world would be somewhere out in the universe and *ipso facto* have to be regarded as material. Consequently, we can't look skyward, as if toward the boundaries of reality, and wonder where the spiritual realm is up there, although in many spiritual movements there is still an inclination to do that. One consequence is that spirit, to us here, is invisible, seems very immaterial, and is therefore an apparently easy target for skeptics, those who accept only the tangible as real.

Yet, our spiritual and more intuitive sensitivities detect spiritual realities. These spiritual capacities seem to be "inside"; we talk about the "inner" man, "inner" experience, etc. But such terminology becomes a quick and loose way of locating spirit. Spirit is *within*, we say, for we normally cannot imagine any other location for it, since it is clearly not *outside*. Actually, we as spirits should not be "inside" our bodies, as if we might probe surgically deep inside, as Swedenborg and others did, for the seat of the soul. Instead, we should seem not to be in material space at all. We are quite real, but a close examination of where we *are* reduces us to the mystery of our not being *here*. The idea that we are inside the body somewhere is basically an illusion caused by the fact that we see and hear through our senses, as if inside looking out.

Swedenborg, therefore, reverses the trend in Western thought to make matter fundamental and mind only an off-shoot or "epiphenomenon" of matter. In fact, it would be more logical to turn that formula around; matter is an epiphenom-enon of mind, and in particular of the Divine Mind. All the-ologies teach at some point that a person must reject any absolute materialism, but confusion about the differences be-tween spirit and matter may still reign elsewhere in a theol-ogy. For example, many faiths will settle for a standoff: there are both mind and matter, but they are separate and somewhat antagonistic realms. One has to choose between them, as Augustine taught.

Elsewhere in a theology there may be visions of the Sec-ond Coming in which Jesus descends from the sky—as if heaven, a realm supposedly of spirit or mind, were floating above us in physical space. Some supermarket tabloids have pandered to this by publishing stories of demons from under the ground, or NASA astronauts who spotted the angelic realm as they shot by it in outer space (how to see heaven without being a mystic). And, of course, there is the more se-rious and very tragic story of the Heaven's Gate cult, who be-lieved that they could commit suicide and thereby board a spacecraft. Oranges and apples get mixed unconscionably by this kind of cosmology in which millenarian prophecy, or any theological end of the world, becomes physical. The reality of the Christian millennium, according to Swedenborg, is actu-ally spiritual, in accordance with its own nature, and it is bet-ter regarded as an "inner" event, an experience in the realm of mind.

Swedenborg gently points out that locating God and heaven, or the supernatural, anywhere in material space is a result of natural thinking. Natural thinking is a kind of default philosophical position that is typically left unchanged from childhood, for we are born into natural thinking, the lowest and most static concepts, so that we can direct our education into higher levels if we want to. We are not born into angelic thought but need to *choose* it, so that it can become our own outlook, not a gift forced on us. Meanwhile, we need to be given some solid ground on which to stand so that the journey to the light can begin. We, therefore, start at the bottom.

Swedenborg developed a strong sensitivity to the differences between spiritual and natural thinking, and he found many writers and theologies overly committed to natural thinking, though they were not necessarily aware of the fact. He understood that it would not be easy to switch over to spiritual thinking, for what that consists of was largely unknown in his time. Indeed, his own theology can be thought of as an extended course on how to think spiritually.

As if this were not enough to contemplate, Swedenborg wrote about several different levels of reality, not just two. There is a basic spiritual reality that incorporates traditional types of experience and uses a familiar theological vocabulary; it talks about spirit, nature, heaven, hell, and the world as large extended realms with familiar sights and sounds that one can deal with in conventionally known ways. These are the subjects of most religious teaching. His books engage in this level of experience primarily because he sought to produce changes in the religious community around him. He had to show people how their actions and states of mind and heart follow them after death and create very personal consequences for them.

Above this familiar and very human level of experience, but visited by Swedenborg's discussions less frequently, are other levels—ultra-metaphysical states that severely challenge the mind to grasp them and that dispense with any semblance of space and time. At these levels, there is nothing left but God and man, and all are in the same dimensionless place. At the highest level, time is only one moment that embraces all of the past, present, and future, and everything has already happened—the possible origin of many esoteric Eastern philosophies. Everything else, every extended spiritual or natural cosmos that moves through time in an endless succession of moments, is an illusion—but one like the Eastern concept of *maya*, which is a kind of substantial illusion that a person can live in and stub a toe on. Humanity may even be reduced further so that God is the one remaining reality. Each higher level of thought and experience is the inner core of the one below it, and all together covertly impart richness and depth to our thinking, especially as we penetrate more deeply into our own minds, a journey that seems to have no end.

There are a natural state of mind and a spiritual state of mind, and each sees its side of the larger mind with solidity and depth, filled with detail and even embedded clues to its ancient past. Archeology and cosmology have given the world and the universe a past that extends eons before the birth of the observer, but that past is derived from appearances that arise from the long history of the larger mind.

Reality looks spiritual when viewed in a spiritual state, natural and static when viewed in a natural state; the observer does not go anywhere to have either experience. In all cases, we merely shift our mode of consciousness; in fact, when we die, *this is all we do*, according to Swedenborg. Nobody goes anywhere at death, for at the more basic levels of reality, as we have mentioned, there is no space or time at all.

If these theories are so, then the old tendency to regard spiritual experience as vague, wispy, and ephemeral, while solid reality is seen as natural or material, can be quickly undermined. The spiritual world should be just as real, vivid, and substantial as the natural world, since both experiences arise from the same observing mind, a mind which changes *only* its state. The shift from one state of being to another, however, is experienced as a change in the apparent space and time that either state will present. In other words, the shift will appear to the spirit as if it had gone somewhere else, to another world. In the classic description of a near-death experience, we find a connecting tunnel and an exotic paradise beyond. But the journey through the tunnel is only a shift, usually somewhat unconscious to us (hence the darkness and the reduced level of sensation in the tunnel), to the other fundamental mode of consciousness.

What is left the same through the change is an enormous similarity of forms. As Carl Jung also discovered, the psyche has its own vocabulary of forms, and a person finds these forms in both spiritual and natural experience. If we can hurt our toes when we kick a rock in this world, it should follow that there is a rock and a vulnerable toe of ours in the spiritual world as well, and the spirit may not be able to detect the difference without looking around for some special defining side effect. According to Swedenborg, one such defining difference is that the meaning of kicking a rock, and what caused a person to do it, will be different. In the spiritual world, the meaning and the cause will both be spiritual.

Solidity is a relationship between a perceived object and the sense that perceives it. It is not an absolute characteristic of anything, even in physics. Our material senses find the material world solid because the senses that view or feel it are also material. Like will see and experience like and regard it as substantial. Given spiritual senses, the world that they perceive will also be spiritual, and that world's relationship to our spiritual senses will thereby produce a solid reality. That fact can create confusion for people who have recently died. Swedenborg encountered many persons who had recently died and were completely unprepared to recognize that they had passed on.

One can also consider the simple fact that all things are perceived by the mind in either case. Behind our simple sense apparatus is the mind, the only actual perceiver of anything. How this one fact might determine the nature of the reality we see is then a very intriguing question. The thing that a mind would most likely experience as solid and real to itself is just more mind, not something strange to itself. Mind should normally perceive as vague and ephemeral that which is other than itself and therefore somewhat strange, having an unclear or chaotic logic. Perceiving some realm as a result of slipping into one of its own modes, spiritual or natural, the mind should find a solid world with clearly defined parts and objects.

This kind of approach can substantially challenge conventional theories. For example, science has in recent times tried to explain how mind arose from matter by suggesting that, if matter gets very complex, as it does in the human nervous system, it can finally generate mind. That is still a very incomplete thesis, constantly poked at in secular literature. It is a theoretical assumption, and it leans on mysterious processes that, under the guise of mere complexity, are supposed to be able to create something out of nothing.

There are serious problems with such assumptions. Swedenborg pointed out that a person cannot logically generate more from the initial starting point than is there to start with; higher entities or forces, such as mind, can't be created from the more mundane, the less capacious. Although we can make what is there more convoluted, tangled, or complex, the final product should be identifiable in its original state, merely a more complicated or more intricate form of the same thing. The final result of such scientific theorizing, he wrote, can be only "continuous with effects." To solve the problem of mind versus matter, we must suggest a higher kind of "stuff" that is not characteristic of material things and can extract them from some of its own properties.

Mind as the primary stuff of reality works better than matter as the primary stuff for at least the following reason: if mind is a manifestation of matter, then the rug is pulled out from under science itself. Science could only with some trouble avoid the possibility that its own ideas may be determined by preset forces in the matter it theorizes about. The result of arguing that matter is the real stuff of existence is a tendency to argue or theorize in a grand circle: we study the material world, but our observations are made by a mind that is only an epiphenomenon, a kind of illusion, created by the material central nervous system, which is in turn merely part of the material world that we are studying. According to classical physics, the material world is very deterministic and has its own implacable agenda. Therefore, it must be calling all the shots in the mental operations of scientists, for it can determine what we think or see.

Consequently, if mind is an offspring of matter, we cannot be sure that the mind is not being ordered around by the current state of its parent and ultimate boss, the physical world. We may be preprogrammed by the world to think in certain ways under certain conditions, including thinking that mind is an epiphenomenon of matter. The mind would have no objectivity that it could rely on.

The idea that lies implicitly behind much of the scientific enterprise, if it is worked out in detail, is that the mind is actually independent of matter. One logical reason for this is the fact that, if science is to be trusted, the scientist must be able to observe the world objectively without having his or her thinking controlled by the deterministic processes that are being studied. This requirement has been overlooked in many skeptical philosophies based on classical physics.

There is an even more basic point that should be kept in mind when dealing with ideas in science that are skeptical about spirit. The traditional thesis that everything real is material may be forced by the belief that science requires material explanations and can't entertain any possibility of the supernatural—that is, anything higher or *prior* to nature. We often hear that everything has a natural explanation. Those words have evolved into a faith that is routinely brought down on the back of paranormal experience, for the statement is not a fact that anyone has ever proven. Instead, in the philosophy of science, a relatively new academic discipline in which the scientific mind and its procedures are analyzed and codified, the statement is referred to as a *methodological imperative.*[5] A methodological imperative is a principle that defines the boundaries of work in the natural sciences; it disciplines its method so that different kinds of work that require different

[5]Students of religion and theology should study the philosophy of science, for it clarifies many mental operations that are useful for both spiritual thought and scientific thought. Swedenborg surreptitiously added much to the field. Because of this relatively new field of study, his ideas become very clear in places that otherwise would be difficult to follow.

methods or rules of procedure can be kept distinct and classed as outside the normal run of scientific work. It does not imply that the supernatural should be considered unreal.

Of course, despite all scientific theories and break-throughs, life and consciousness remain mysterious.

As we have mentioned, Swedenborg discovered that the world of mind does look like this one (and near-death experiences suggest that we don't revert to something entirely different when the spirit takes flight). Swedenborg's descriptions of the spiritual world show that it has lakes, rivers, fields, trees, mountains, clouds, a sun and moon, all the "furniture" normal to the material world. The difference is that these things are spiritual. That is, they are forms in which dynamic states of mind and feeling are perceived directly by the observer and therefore in some recognizable form. Indeed, Swedenborg informs us that spirits there look entirely like people—they have arms, legs, a face, and so on.

In his work *Heaven and Hell,* Swedenborg describes the spiritual world most fully, and it can seem at first that he is being much too earthy with such an unearthly realm. Why all the earth imagery? After all, mountains are the result of geophysical processes. Why should spirit mimic the planet Earth? The logic of the situation, he taught, is actually the other way around. It is not that the spiritual world looks like the natural world; the natural world looks like the spiritual world. The shoe has always been on the other foot, since spirit is prior to nature; that is, nature is an expression of spirit, not the other way around. Matter is a relatively static expression of a rather large and comprehensive mind, and to reside in *either* world, as has already been argued, is actually to take up a location that is merely a state of that mind.

Therefore, the trappings of the natural world are in themselves spiritually meaningful, an expression of the inner realm that created them, though that realm is static here, very sluggish in response to our own state of mind and not at all likely to change or disappear as we change our attitudes. Some sense of this spirituality in nature's forms inspires us to look for spiritual refreshment in nature, even though our science doesn't try to explain why we should feel like doing this unless the reasons are arbitrary and subjective.

What distinguishes the two worlds is that in the natural world, and in the natural mode of the mind that perceives it, there is a strong separation of *Self* and *Other*. That creates objective experience, the tendency for spaces in the natural world to be experienced as the same by everybody. If A is a mile from B, everybody sees A as a mile from B. The natural world is always the Other, not the image of the Self. In this way, we become aware of our selves and the presence of an opposing world to act upon in accordance with our wishes, good or bad. We take action, or it seems to take action involving us; and instructive results occur: we are forced to learn basic lessons from these results. The contrast between ourselves and our surroundings creates a strong self-consciousness, which then allows us to become concerned about our condition and to try to develop our intelligence and ability to deal with a clearly non-empathetic world. Our self-consciousness, in turn, leads to ethics and problems in discipline and practical wisdom. This world is, therefore, an ideal learning environment, a goad to consciousness, as if we were given a model of spiritual reality with which we can play and experiment without also taking messy risks with our inner selves.

In the spiritual world, however, the situation is different: everything, including people, is related to everything else. The spiritual world is always a whole, not a bunch of detached parts. It is a world of vast, interpenetrating relationships, and it operates like one very large mind—all minds taken as a whole, though the Divine Mind permeates and orders the collective mind. If things have gone well, concern for others replaces concentration on oneself, and the spirit becomes part of the whole of humanity, no longer facing everyone or everything else as the Other. Since the spiritual world essentially consists of a group conciousness, it logically follows the earlier worldly effort to define oneself first and become a distinct individual, a "somebody" in particular. When a spirit has defined who he or she is, the spirit can enter constructively into intimate relationships with others and not be overwhelmed by them. Thus, once again, the natural world prepares one for the spiritual world.

Swedenborg points out that any group or relationship is only as strong as the individuals within it have independently learned to be. Therefore, the formation and education of individuals in the physical world must precede their entrance into the special dynamics of the spiritual world. This looks paradoxical, for it has seemed that the difference, distinctiveness, and self-reliance that a person enjoys would resist real unity with others. In this material world, we have seen too many individualists go off by themselves. We have also seen idealistic spiritual movements that promote the opposite, that teach that its members should merge with the group and everyone believe and think alike. Such groups teach the surrender of individuality in order to bring about complete sharing and empathy, a common mind. That would seem to save society from the impact of our arrogant individualism. But it usually results only in a group without backbone and consciousness, since everyone leans on everyone else. The situation then demands that a brain be added who can direct something so amorphous. The teacher or guru then imposes him- or herself on the group as its brain and treats the group as if it were a private army, able to work, provide services, and give pleasures at the guru's whim. The result is a cult.

Swedenborg, on the other hand, wrote that, in all truly unified groups and societies, everyone is "one distinctly." In this kind of ethic, cults cannot grow, because everyone brings in a well-developed individuality and has a unique role to play in a larger whole, the wise pursuit of which is his or her responsibility; all of these roles taken together form a single collective mind. The brain of the group is everybody. An entire society, made up of "myriads" of such people, is seen in heaven, and at a distance, as a single person. In one beautiful experience, Swedenborg saw an entire heavenly society as many stars that came together to form a large individual. Each person knows his or her capacities very well and is, therefore, also aware of personal limits and when to give way to someone else.

One consequence of this pervasive emphasis on relationships in the other world is that what is seen may look somewhat different the next time we see it, but its appearance will be a function of its nature plus any changes in our relationship to it. Taken by itself, that may seem strange and disorienting; but it is, in fact, the way we have always functioned in our own psychology. We are used to regarding the same things differently at different times, taking up a myriad of different attitudes and seeing things differently, depending on how we feel or on how the situation we are in has changed. Distance in the spiritual world is what we experience here as psychological distance. To be far away from someone there is to be in a very different state of mind and heart. To be close by someone there is to be more intimately related to him or her. We know all this as a reality in our psychology, but in this world it does not affect our senses. In the other world it does.

At first, after death, the spirit finds this new world strange, but its psychological familiarity soon settles in. What has to settle in is only the perception that our old psychological states are now showing up outside rather than just "inside." The spiritual world quickly becomes the most natural one to live in, because it merely surrounds us with our old, accustomed psychology. The relatively cold remoteness of natural things is replaced by our intimacy with mind itself, and this leads on to a deeper intimacy with people around us.

Swedenborg once encountered a man in the spiritual world who was standing in midair a little above the ground. Although the man had to look down at him, he was entirely unconscious that he was levitating, and he went on to tell Swedenborg about his skepticism that there was any life at all after death, an ironic opinion for a man of his elevated position to bring up. Rather than debate him, Swedenborg merely pointed to where he was standing. The man looked down, suddenly awoke from his airy theorizing and ran off in fright, but for the moment not yet back on solid ground.

In the spirit's fantasy-ridden state of mind, he could not keep both feet on the ground in that kind of world, and so his physical condition reflected that psychological fact. The ground there represents the practical mind, the most functional and "grounded" aspects of daily thought. The spirit had literally floated off in an absorbing reverie about his ideas, too occupied to notice that he was acting out his detached state of mind while reciting theories that denied his actual experience. In the other world, where inner states become the dominant physics and are dramatized, such denial amounts literally to ungrounded thinking. As he saw how much fantasy he was entertaining, he got more down to earth.

Swedenborg points out, undoubtedly with a wry smile, that many common metaphors, like the ones above, are from the spiritual world. We think to some extent "spiritually" without knowing it because we sense a remarkable appropriateness in certain terms and phrases. The spirit seems to recognize its own language, though its remarkable suitability remains unanalyzed, too instinctual to attract our attention.

For example, in this world, we say, "We are very close," to indicate a feeling of mutual attraction or sympathy. In the spiritual world we are literally very close—in some instances touching. "We are no longer as close as we used to be" becomes in the spiritual world real distance from the other person, even though they are sitting together in this world. "I see what you mean" may in the spiritual world be accompanied by the sudden appearance of an object or view that had been invisible before. In this other world, the spirit understands and therefore sees. Furthermore, heat is love; the "cold heart" applies especially to people who live in cold climates in that world. They are actually frozen by their own hardness of heart but are probably continuing to blame it on the weather.

Furthermore, Swedenborg explained, disagreement occasions disappearance. When two spirits or two different crowds with opposing views encounter each other, an argument may make each side vanish from the other. Here in this world we say, "I don't see your point at all." If the disagreement is complete and passionate, the houses and possessions of the other side may also vanish, indicating that the one side doesn't understand that frame of mind at all, so its opponents disappear with all of their inner furniture. Here in this world, we can see this happening in our minds, even though our senses do not suddenly record a lot of special effects. In either world, someone may tell us, "I don't know you anymore." In the spiritual world, the inner landscape closes up so that nothing involved in the dispute is visible. You can't defeat the phenomenon by going around and feeling for invisible people or houses there, because the invisibility is a part of your own state of mind, not an objective invisibility. It indicates complete rejection of the reality of the other state of mind.

These activities in the spiritual world may seem suffocatingly subjective, a product of one's own illusions of thought and expectation. But Swedenborg points out that those who love the truth and are open to it see what *really* is the case. The higher regions, closer to the Divine, who is Love itself and Wisdom itself, are therefore more stable, much more revealing. Truth holds erratic egoism on a steadier course, giving it an inner reference point. The higher a spirit goes in the spiritual world, the more he or she sees in the light of spiritual truth, compared to what Swedenborg calls the "fatuous" light of fantasy and egoistic expectation.

The Divine is seen only in heaven, for heaven is the state in which spiritual consciousness and mutual love are so well developed that the Divine can be seen usually in daily experience—precisely as spiritually evolved people claim to do here. In the highest level of heaven, the Divine appears as a brilliant sun, whose light is truth and whose heat is love. Love and wisdom frequently appear that way. Some appearances that are similar to this are recorded in near-death experiences where the person sees a brilliant light that does not hurt the eyes.

Swedenborg's experience of the spiritual world suggests an explanation for the visions of psychics that great natural disasters lie in wait for us at the millennium. If there is anything that is common to the predictions of Scripture and the visions of psychics and prophets of the last days, it is bad news: earthquakes, mountains sinking into the sea, desolation, the end of the world as we know it. Why should it be this way?

As we have seen, Swedenborg found that the material world is a reflection of the spiritual. Therefore, any such prediction of impending destruction may not have anything to do with our mountains, for the spiritual world has mountains as well. Mountains are original features there, the essence of all mountains, special aspects or forms of *mind*; in our world, there are only static reflections of these living mountains. Indeed, Swedenborg wrote that spiritual transformation is definitely the import of apocalyptic statements in Scripture. The biblical apocalypse is not a statement about the physical world, but indicates great changes in human consciousness and attitudes. The world of the psyche or soul is the subject of the apocalypse. The new heaven and the new earth that are supposed to exist after the Last Judgment are not a new universe and a new planet. They are meaningful only as symbols of inner change.

Visions of earthquakes that will sink mountains or the coastline and raise old civilizations out of the water sometime near the millennium, as in Edgar Cayce's predictions, could very well be images of accustomed values that are dying and being replaced with an older wisdom. References to California and other worldly locations don't tie us to a material interpretation. Swedenborg points out that representations exist in the spiritual world—special images of specific things that suit current states of mind or expectation. London and other great cities have their counterparts in the world of spirits (where everyone goes immediately after death), though they are not strictly identical to the earthly cities. Residents of a country find themselves in familiar places after death, surrounded by other citizens and buildings with at least the same general character as the worldly ones. Old culture survives death in the hearts of those who pass on, and it produces experiences that look and feel much the same as those of its physical counterpart.

For example, Atlantis or other ancient civilizations rising from the deep may be interpreted as the return of ancient wisdom coming back into mind, rising above the waters of modern neglect. Whether Atlantis actually existed, an endless bone of contention, doesn't matter to the language of representative terms and images. Whatever each of these things means to the psychic will be a valid term in the language of representation. Swedenborg discovered that an angel will always communicate with a person in his or her own language. Let a New Age psychic view the future, and he or she will find it spelled out in whatever terminology and imagery the New Age community has been using. As we have mentioned above, Swedenborg's basic rule in interpreting spiritual imagery is that everything in the spiritual world is experienced as a reflection of the observer's state of mind.

Now if all this is true, then apocalyptic visions would be better explained as calls to the faithful to acknowledge new shifts in consciousness and trust them to be real. They help the psychic and his or her audience to move ahead into new awareness and their required changes. Otherwise, human inertia cautions too many of us to hold back for safety's sake and not enter a new age. The mind does not normally want to be transformed, because change looks like an entrance into chaos or strangeness. We often remain with the inconveniences of old ideas and conceptions, old habits, not because we know that they are better, but because they are comfortable.

It may not be clear that an apocalyptic vision *is* really about the future. In fact, the only reason for thinking that it does depict the future is that the catastrophe—say the sinking of California's coastline—has not yet happened. So much about the timing of these events in the still mysterious future, and the fateful dilemmas of millenarian movements (such as Jehovah's Witnesses) seems to be driven solely by literalism, the perennially unchallenged conviction that the Bible and psychic visions are always to be taken at face value. The belief constitutes the dubious strategy of putting all of one's eggs in one basket without seeing if such portentous things might have other interpretations. If these visions are symbolic representations, not views of material future events, they may very well be happening now. The biblical predictions may even have been fulfilled already.

Therefore, what millenarian prophecies may reveal is a renaissance, not a catastrophe. They may be covert clues that things are already getting better. Oddly enough, apocalyptic upheavals, if merely taken inwardly, may be great news.

Whatever Scripture says about the last times, the portrayal must depict some process that is natural to spiritual growth and does not bring divine imperatives, such as the continual need to bring all to God's kingdom, to an end. Some shift in the way we think about Scripture and about theology needs to take place. A strict literal reading of the Bible satisfies only the dogmatic mind that is determined to be obedient, even at the expense of spiritual wisdom. Swedenborg was vividly aware of this. His vision of the Last Judgment is based on his theology of a God that is absolute Love and Wisdom.

God, he taught, produced two distinct worlds—the celestial and the natural, or heaven and earth—in order to create people to love. There can be as many people as there are aspects of the divine character itself, an infinite number. Each of us is designed to be a reflection of one of these infinitely numerous appearances of divinity so that the Divine can dwell with that aspect of himself in each of us. Moreover, the appearances of divinity continue in the heavenly realm after our life on earth, so that heaven can become infinitely large, since each new self who enters it enlarges it with his or her own mind or self. The landscape of this earth is finite, but that of heaven is infinitely expandable since there is no limit to how large the collective mind can become.

The Divine who lives within each of us and within the totality of all of us is Love itself and Wisdom itself;

Swedenborg argues that these divine qualities are "substantial," that is, they are self-sustaining, not abstractions or states of something else. Together they constitute a Person, and reality is alive. God is a Person, and we only receive and contain love and wisdom. We are small images of it.

With this concept of a self-sustaining love and wisdom, Swedenborg opposes the often unconscious tendency in many theologies to think of God as a being who only *possesses* love and wisdom. That idea, that there is a possessor, allows the possibility that the possessor is still evolving and is not yet perfectly aligned with the love and wisdom inside. A self that only has love and wisdom as states of itself must be postulated because we are used to thinking of love and wisdom only as states of some kind of underlying substance. But as the source of love and wisdom, not a mere possessor, God would not destroy any portion of himself; as images of his vast variety, we are, in effect, a part of the Divine. Unlike God, however, we are mere possessors of love and wisdom.

Everything, Swedenborg wrote, was created by Wisdom from Love, and religion can only make Love and Wisdom the essential reality. Here we return for a moment to a previous discussion. The material world is only a derivative state, a set of systematically arranged appearances dependent on the general state of the lesser mind (or the human mind) that observes them, and are intended for its growth into love and wisdom. We don't think in these terms, however, and we take the reality of the outer world for granted. And for most purposes this works fine. But now suppose that the divine Love and Wisdom were to stop maintaining the natural mind, were to withdraw its actions. The universe would simply vanish— no thunder, no drama, no special effects that most apocalyptic dramas envision.

A God that is Love and Wisdom, however, would not be interested in pulling the plug, as it were. Swedenborg points out that maintenance is perpetual creation. The universe is continually being re-created. It is not a stable entity that can persist on its own for even one second, although that fact systematically eludes us; the only reality, Love and Wisdom, maintains a convenient, rapidly recurring illusion, *maya,* which our lesser minds take for granted. God, however, is a self-subsisting mind. As such, God, as Love and Wisdom, wants to maintain, not destroy.

CHAPTER VII

THE HIDDEN MILLENNIUM

With Swedenborg's ideas in the background, we can now comment more coherently on problems in interpreting apocalyptic Scripture.

Swedenborg's experiences of the other world were not only instructive introductions to the nature of reality; they also showed him how the Bible was written. Swedenborg believed that the "Word," as he called it, is the most recent and expanded form of an ancient revelation that was passed on originally by a love of instructive storytelling. The earliest spiritual societies depicted great spiritual themes in material garb, putting complex and subtle psychological and spiritual ideas into the form of human dramas that turned the world into a mythic stage. Even material objects seemed to be forms of spiritual things. In this way the world became alive to them.

Elsewhere in the Word, in historical dramas written long after these early and consciously mythic writers had disappeared, the stories in Scripture became more mundane, more like ordinary history. Swedenborg states that these later stories were based on real people, and they were sometimes more, sometimes less, faithful to literal fact; but they still possessed the same patterns, the same progressions from one state to another, as might be described in a profound, literal text on trends and patterns in spiritual psychology. The sacred texts providentially continued to be inwardly significant, possessing a systematic "inner sense."

Thus, Swedenborg learned, the stories in biblical history merely mimic the events of the growth or decline of the soul, or of human spirituality and consciousness. This is what Swedenborg meant by the inner sense in the Word—not a metaphysical sense, revealing secrets of the universe, or some kind of occult knowledge, but pure spiritual psychology. The Word extended its insights to great depths, and it merely used the imagery of the material world and the events of history to present its theses. Material events and characters are its external vocabulary.

This is the reason that people can read the Bible, even in passages with a soap-opera mix of values and a cast of horrendously flawed characters, yet find fascination and a very subtle—and sometimes not-so-subtle—healing power. The reader is mysteriously refreshed without knowing why, even in chapters that deal solely with statistics and laws, ceremonial rules, and the genealogy of families. Outwardly, much of the Bible looks very mundane, is not even a logical or chronological story. But the soul of the devout reader, for some reason, feels that it is being fed, even in these places. The reason is that the soul responds subconsciously to models of its own inner life, even when there is no conscious awareness that such models are being shown.

Swedenborg explained that, as a man or woman reads the text very literally, the angels understand spiritually and respond from the heavens. Because of this, the reader and the heavens are joined, bringing healing to the human being and joy over the connection to the heavens. Even deeper inside, each story teaches about the Lord and the actions of divine love and wisdom, the fundamental contents of angelic consciousness.

As if to warn people who might simply rely on his readings of the inner sense for scriptural instruction, Swedenborg pointed out that there is still no substitute for reading the Word directly, that is, with the literal imagery intact; no other book could duplicate its ability to communicate with heaven through its own language and imagery. For this, the imagery must remain hidden, in mind. In fact, Swedenborg's own writings, despite their painstaking efforts to be explanatory in more philosophical and analytical ways, did not communicate with the heavens. Only what we see as the very literal and material sense of the Word could be spiritually revealing to the angels.[1] Study of the literal sense, as if for its own sake, remains a mandate for Christians, for it is written in a language that the angels readily transform into their own thoughts. Despite this, Swedenborg still advises the reader not to take the literal sense as the essential reality.

Biblical history in its purely literal aspects often constitutes the ethical side of religion, the level of teaching that formulates rules of behavior in specific kinds of situations. These rules produce practical wisdom about how to govern our actions in response to the challenges of physical existence and spiritual living. While we have these stories for our ethical instruction, the angels respond to the same text on a higher level, with an internal wisdom, a more psychological and spiritual understanding that often explains why the worldly ethic is mandated in the literal sense. The transaction ties the spiritual community on earth to the one in heaven and makes them of one mind, even though they are not on the same level of consciousness. Swedenborg says that the two levels "correspond" to each other. He also points out that, if we dispose our outer lives and our conscious decisions well, the Lord will arrange our inner selves accordingly. The difference between the various levels of understanding Scripture is a part of this general strategy. Angelic consciousness is built up deep inside

[1] Emanuel Swedenborg, *Concerning the Sacred Scripture of the Word of the Lord from Experience* (*De Verbo*), ¶ 47–48, in *Posthumous Theological Works*, vol. 1, tr. John Whitehead, 2nd edition (West Chester, Pennsylvania: Swedenborg Foundation, 1996).

as we obey the ethical injunctions and practical implications of the literal stories.

For Swedenborg, the central meaning of the Christian millennium, the Second Coming of the Lord, was a coming of new light and consciousness through an awareness of the multiple levels of meaning in the Word—and, therefore, in the human soul that it covertly models, the inner angelic mind and the outer natural mind. The Bible is a model of the depths of the soul in which God dwells, and understanding the model necessarily points us to the inner spiritual reality that it represents, waking us up to it. By exposing our conscious thoughts to the Word's inner meanings, he said, we may now open up the corresponding higher levels of the soul and see what previous theologians had speculated about. We may now approach the level of understanding that the angels enjoy— but only if we read in the right spirit and grow spiritually:

> The reason why it is hurtful to confirm the apparent truth of the Word to the point of destroying the genuine truth that lies hidden within is that each and all things of the sense of the letter of the Word communicate with heaven, and open it. . . . So that when a man applies this sense to confirm loves of the world that are contrary to loves of heaven, the internal of the Word is made false. The result is that when its external of the sense of the letter, and which now has a false internal, communicates with heaven, heaven is closed; for the angels, who are in the internal of the Word, reject that particular external conception of it. Thus it is evident that a false internal, or truth falsified, takes away communication with heaven and closes heaven. This is why it is hurtful to confirm any heretical falsity.[2]

Swedenborg did not stop with theory about the inner sense, but provided very thorough demonstrations. In his monumental twelve-volume study *Arcana Coelestia* (Heavenly Secrets), he explains the inner meaning of the books of Gen-

[2]Emanuel Swedenborg, *Doctrine of Sacred Scripture*, ¶ 96, in *Four Doctrines*, tr. John Faulkner Potts, 2nd edition (West Chester, Pennsylvania: Swedenborg Foundation, 1997).

esis and Exodus, virtually word by word. Later, he provided a similar study of the book of Revelation, *Apocalypse Revealed*, showing that it describes not the end of the world, but the end of a "church" or religious dispensation, and the birth of a new one. The old Christian consciousness, a world in itself, was in his time beginning to be replaced by a new one, "a new heaven and a new earth," that could take Christendom to a higher level and give it new life. The transformation could take place only in the inner life of man, the spiritual world, where everyone, living or dead, is gathered together as depicted in the Last Judgment drama.

Swedenborg made no effort to found a separate church, probably because the current Christian institutions possessed the Word with its massive ethical wisdom and would need only to be reformed over time by better thinking on higher levels and about matters of principle. He was prepared to apply a virtually Buddhist patience to that long, slow, rethinking process. Otherwise, Christian culture was well developed and entrenched, and there was no need to reinvent it.

How does such a revolution in biblical interpretation look, once it is laid out in any detail? We can now turn to Swedenborg's detailed explanation of the millennium, as contained in two works, *Apocalypse Revealed* and *The Last Judgment and Babylon Destroyed*.

In *The Last Judgment*, Swedenborg explains that a "dispensation," or religious era, declines in time as the accumulated evil of its members builds up and its original visions are dimmed. Eventually, a general reordering has to take place, followed by the establishment of a new religious era. Each time this happens, the era and its "church" or spirituality is subjected to a "last judgment." Swedenborg argues that the Last Judgment can take place only where everyone who would be affected is gathered together, therefore, in the spiritual world, not here on earth, for the gathering brings together the spirits of the living and the dead. Its object is to separate good from evil so that the two are not confused with each other and can be recognized without misleading appearances. Because this is a spiritual event, a clarifying event in the realm of mind, it is actually a shift in the quality of human consciousness, both in the other world and in our own lives. Afterwards, our spiritual choices become clearer, and anyone who so wishes can become wise much more readily.

A judgment is imposed only on the spiritual community, however. An important implication of Swedenborg's thought is that judgment is passed only on the religious community that was supposed to guide the era; it never falls as punishment on the world as a whole. Besides, punishment makes little sense if the Divine is not recognized by everyone at some beginning point. Those parts of humanity that have cultivated spiritual consciousness will be visited, for they have become responsible for their spiritual mission.

It is also pointless to call everything to a halt and lose those who might eventually be saved by the religious community. The Divine loves everyone personally, even the evil, who also always have the capacity to change their ways. The individual is primarily conscious of his or her own need for relationship with something. In the traditional apocalyptic drama, where everyone perishes—good and evil, young and old, all the living who always have the potential to reform—the Christian ideal of a personal and loving God disappears.

Conventional millennial theologies suggest that God has given up on the human race as a whole and does not contemplate creating any new order or cosmos. He will simply retire with the few people he has won as if he is in retreat, regretting his original decision to start the world and conceding defeat to Satan. And other questions arise. If God can see the future, why did he not see what would happen to his decision to create humanity? This problem is consistent with the literal understanding of the Last Judgment prophecies standard in most churches.

In Swedenborg's vision, the world is to be wooed and hopefully saved, not abandoned, and efforts to do so are always the implacable intentions of divine love. The "last days" are best understood as the last states of an old consciousness, as God brings himself once again within range of human aspirations and renews the spiritual mind.

On a more universal stage, God cannot stop creating people to love and bring to himself, and therefore the generations will never come to an end. Swedenborg writes,

> *That the procreations of the human race will endure to eternity is plain from many considerations, of which some are shown in the work on Heaven [and Hell], especially from the following:*
>
> *I. The human race is the basis on which heaven is founded.*
>
> *II. The human race is the seminary of heaven.*
>
> *III. The extension of heaven, which is for angels, is so immense that it cannot be filled to eternity.*
>
> *IV. They are but few respectively, of whom heaven at present is formed.*
>
> *V. The perfection of heaven increases according to its numbers.*
>
> *VI. And every Divine work has respect to infinity and eternity. . . .*
>
> *The angelic heaven is the end for which all things in the universe were created, for it is the end on account of which the human race exists, and the human race is the end regarded in the creation of the visible heaven, and the earths included in it. Wherefore that divine work, namely, the angelic heaven, primarily has respect to infinity and eternity, and therefore to its multiplication without end, for the divine himself dwells therein. Hence also it is clear that the human race will never cease, for were it to cease, the divine work would be limited to a certain number, and thus its looking to infinity would perish.*[3]

[3] *The Last Judgment and Babylon Destroyed,* ¶ 7; 13, in *Miscellaneous Theological Works,* tr. John Whitehead, 2nd edition (West Chester, Pennsylvania: Swedenborg Foundatin, 1996). This work has also been translated in more contemporary English by George Dole, under the title *The Last Judgment in Retrospect* (1996); it too is published by the Swedenborg Foundation.

As a scientist, Swedenborg leaves room for the eventual end of the planet, which may have its own very long lifetime and a natural end, as do all things in nature. But the universe, which has many inhabited planets in it, is continually productive. The cosmic picture implies that, although planets have a limited lifetime, others capable of being inhabited are continually created. It is the universal cycle of generations that cannot stop. In this cosmic perspective, it becomes clear that God will continue to create the human race and to save it. Therefore, he does not give up on his creation.

If a Last Judgment is not physical but spiritual, then one may have already happened, or may very well happen, at any time. Once again we encounter the effects of literalism—if the Bible is supposed to be taken literally, then we cannot avoid putting the Last Judgment in the future, since the world is still here. Swedenborg tells us that a judgment on the Christian church, predicted in the Gospels and Revelation, did take place—in 1757. He observed it in the spiritual world and published descriptions of it in his *Last Judgment*, published in 1758. His private diary,[4] covering the period from 1746 to 1765, also contains many accounts of it.

Several judgments have occurred, one for each major religious era in human history. As we have mentioned, a judgment divides one major development in spiritual consciousness from another and allows the next era to begin, after which the inevitable decline occurs and the process has to be repeated. Swedenborg was told that the Bible contains especially vivid predictions of both the end of the Judaic era and the end of the first Christian era. The prophets foretold the earlier judgment, and the Gospels and the book of Revelation foretold the next one. A new, clarified order was to follow each one. The predictions of the end of the Judaic era are as apocalyptic as the predictions of the Last Judgment in Christian scriptures and involve similar imagery:

[4]Emanuel Swedenborg, *The Spiritual Diary*, (London: Swedenborg Society, 1977). This work was published posthumously.

Behold, the cruel day of Jehovah cometh; the stars of the heavens and the constellations thereof shall not shine with their light, the sun shall be darkened at his rising, and the moon shall not cause her light to shine.

ISAIAH 12:9,10

When I shall put thee out, I will cover the heavens, and make the stars thereof dark; I will cover the sun with a cloud, and the moon shall not cause her light to shine, and I will give darkness upon thy land.

EZEKIEL 22:7,8

The day of Jehovah cometh, a day of darkness, the sun and moon shall not cause their light to shine, and the stars shall withdraw their shining.

JOEL 2:1,2,10

The sun shall be turned into darkness, and the moon into blood, before the great clay of Jehovah cometh (3:4). The day of Jehovah is near in the valley of decision; the sun and moon are darkened.

JOEL 4:14,15

Swedenborg observed, "In all these passages it treats of the last time of the Jewish Church, which was when the Lord came into the world." In the very similar apocalyptic imagery of the Last Judgment predictions in Matthew, the afflicted sun is love, the moon is faith, and the stars that shall fall to the earth are the "knowledges" of good and truth. He added, "By the above, therefore, collected into one sense, is meant, that there would be no love, nor faith, nor knowledges of good and truth, remaining in the Christian Church, in the last time when it draws to its end."[5]

Notice that the stars falling to earth are not divinely caused, as anyone would have to suppose in a literal reading;

[5] *Brief Exposition of the Doctrine of the New Church*, ¶ 78 in *Miscellaneous Theological Works*, tr. John Whitehead, 2nd edition (West Chester, Pennsylvania: Swedenborg Foundation, 1996).

only God can bring the universe down on our heads. In a literal reading, the apocalypse is pictured as a physical crisis produced by God, evidently in great wrath. Such cosmic destruction and such a vengeful God do not agree with a God of love and reason. If, however, we regard the description as symbolic, the imagery may be applied to the religious mind and how it sees its own cosmos. When the collective religious mind fails itself and others and unduly affects the world around itself, it brings the stars down, for its own decline has failed to keep the stars of faith in place. False ideas have emptied its view of the heavens—the higher mind—and that brings on a purification.

Why was the religious era in which Swedenborg lived ripe for judgment? Swedenborg reconstructs some of Christianity's early history somewhat in the following vein:

When the Lord came to earth, people were not ready for very high states of spiritual illumination, so the Christian church became a movement of mixed ideals and much uncertainty. The brotherhood that held that movement together in its early years was based on simple faith and a love that was largely confined to the members of the movement, not a truly advanced love of humanity based on universal principles.

In his parable of the tares (Matt. 13:24–30), Jesus taught that an enemy would come and scatter the seeds of tares among the wheat. The time of harvest, a time representing judgment, would require that both the wheat and the tares be allowed to grow up together, lest the wheat—the children of God—be uprooted along with the tares. When the field had grown ripe, the tares could be rooted out, allowing the wheat to stand apart and be harvested separately. This parable forecast complex spiritual problems that would characterize the Christian era before a second and final cleansing and clarification of the Christian viewpoint could take place.

These problems have included incomplete or inconsistent spiritual ideals, obscure and dangerously misleading concepts of God, naturalistic thinking, destructive quarrels between denominations, narrow concepts of the neighbor who is to be loved, and a misunderstanding of what salvation means. A persistent tendency to darkness hung on to challenge or block Christians again and again, inducing the rather cloudy history of a Christian church seduced by the attractions of political and military power. One of the worst symptoms of a spiritual malaise was, of course, the Inquisition.

In the last centuries before 1757, the Lord was considered to be merely one of a trinity of divine persons, whereas the original perception of God was simpler and much more effective spiritually—the Trinity existed in the Lord as three aspects of himself. God had come to earth to relate more visibly to his people. In heaven, Swedenborg observed in his many heavenly visits, no one is worshipped except the Lord. The idea of three persons in the Trinity came dangerously close to being an idea of three gods. This delicate boundary of heretical theory, he argued, was actually often crossed, though the fact was never acknowledged.

Salvation was finally supposed to be obtained by mere belief in the Lord (the doctrine of faith alone) without the necessary presence of a good life, in effect allowing hypocrisy to enter the church. Good works were basically signs of faith, and faith or belief—that is, according to whatever theology or religious sect a person followed—was responsible for actually saving the individual, not good works. Swedenborg argued that a changed life, new practical values, a genuine desire to love others actively, are necessary for real repentance, or the purported faith does not actually exist. The heart, more deeply examined, turns out to be cold.

Many Christians by Swedenborg's time were backing away from a belief in a spiritual world and were even skeptical about the existence of an independent soul. Naturalism, the elevation of nature as the fundamental reality, was moving ever more critically toward the center of Christian thought. The Christian message was dying from the inside out, and the results, to his privileged eye, could be seen in the spiritual world.

In Jesus' time, the need for a judgment and a new era could already be spelled out, even though Jesus' coming was itself such a judgment on an old and rigid spirituality. The Second Coming, the second judgment that would affect Christian history, was forecast in great detail in the book of Revelation only a few years afterwards, which is filled with dramatic detail and stunningly beautiful symbolic images that depict a complex process of cleansing and renewal. To Swedenborg, the book of Revelation is the logical continuation of the parable of the tares. Christianity had to be established in two major stages. The second stage, which has been building slowly over the years since 1757, would see a more clear-thinking spiritual community rising quietly in various places.

As was mentioned in the previous chapter, Swedenborg did not think it necessary to found a new institution to represent this new era. He instead sent his books to existing churches and institutions in the hope that the new perspectives would filter down to society everywhere from already existing points of distribution. Bishops and the nobility were common recipients of his books, as was the general reading public, since his message was not limited to a privileged few. His strategy was always to work from the inside of society out, not from the outside in. The new ground for a field clear of tares was everywhere, and he evidently felt that it would grow itself, given half a chance.

In the meantime, old religious denominations would continue, and governments and the ordinary affairs of daily life would go on; but new wisdom would become available for all who genuinely wanted to achieve it. These people Swedenborg called the New Church.[6]

What may also need to be understood in our own very troubled time is that the disease that killed the old Christian era was spiritual indifference, the lack of awareness of crisis.

[6] The reader should remember that a "church" to Swedenborg was not a church *per se*, a religious institution, but a new religious character.

There is some hope if people can see that crisis exists and try to recover.

No time was more purposely oblivious to spiritual crisis than the eighteenth century. Thomas Carlyle, the Victorian cultural theorist, wrote of it in his *Frederick the Great*:

> *A century which has no history and can have little or none. A century so opulent in accumulated falsities . . . as never century before was! Which had no longer the consciousness of being false, so false had it grown; and was so steeped in falsity, and impregnated with it to the very bone, that—in fact the measure of the thing was full, and a French Revolution had to end it. . . . A very fit termination, as I thankfully feel, for such a century. . . . For there was need once more of a Divine Revelation to the torpid, frivolous children of men, if they were not to sink altogether into the ape condition.*

When living a good life is not considered to be the most important in achieving salvation, then the Christian community is headed for spiritual indifference because its true heart is no longer evident. Swedenborg declared that, in his time, the declining church had entered a state of indifference after moving out of a more dangerous period in which it could receive the truth but would then reverse itself and reject it, mixing truth with false beliefs until the difference between them could not be detected. This would have amounted to a profanation of the truth, and it is very dangerous to the soul. The final period of indifference was merciful, for it did not include the possibility of profaning the truth. But it could only precede the judgment.

During such times when a community loses touch with its essential truths, religious ceremony replaces moral action, and support of the institution replaces caring among individuals. True worship, Swedenborg pointed out, is regeneration—change for the better in terms of an individual's life and morals, motivated by an actual love of what is better. A person must take on the stress of change, resisting temptations to do worse; such action allows God to work inside and change the human will.

In all times, it is customary to deplore contemporary conditions. In the present time, however, we have faced the prospect, unlike any other, of nothing less than nuclear annihilation. We also face the disintegration of values in the home and in society in general, the loss of our natural environment to corporate greed, and the rise of autocratic governments that cannot grasp the spirit of international cooperation.

But new eras are *not* refuted by their problems. New eras are not necessarily going to be easy. Problems at such a time can be converted into opportunities for spectacular spiritual growth. For example, as good becomes more prevalent, evil will rise to meet it. It is goaded to come out and oppose its own suffocation. Then it can be pointed out and dealt with. As long as religious or spiritual communities are mobilized by the threats against it and react, and as long as targets for healing are pointed out, they will get whatever help they need from the higher realms.

What Swedenborg saw in the spiritual world was truly apocalyptic:

> That mountain, with the mountains round about, where was a similar religion, sank down from its altitude even to the plane of the horizon, where the [teachers of false ideas] afterwards wandered; nor were they longer able, by looking abroad from the height, to rule over the lands round about; for when they ruled, they did all kinds of evil to those who were not willing to worship them and their deities. . . .

> After the many particular vastations of which I spoke above were accomplished, and those companies, which were many, were thrust down from the mountains and rocks and cast into ponds, marshes, lakes, and gulfs, from which they can never ascend—there came, at length, certain ones who placed themselves above others and incited souls against the Lord and against the Divine Truth which is from Him. From these, the whole mass, as it were, began to be fermented; and it was observed that that disturbance and tumult spread around on every side, in from

ten to twenty mountains and rocks, to those who were upon them and those who were beneath, at the foot and even to the summits, where it was believed the heavens were; for they who were there appeared, to those lower down, like a mist; and it was believed that the heavens were [up] there.

These also . . . got into the tumult; and then some exalted themselves, and the rest attached themselves to them and aided them, for the sole purpose of destroying those who were in Divine Truth from the Lord. When, therefore, attention was turned to the fact that the contagion was spreading on every side, there occurred a general appearance of the Lord. It was like a cloudy sphere, which was borne about upon the mountains and rocks and carried down all the dwellers there.

Those mountains and mountain-tops receded and sank down, some quite to the plain. The cities were cast down, and desolation appeared everywhere. This was the destruction of heaven and earth which, in the genuine sense, is meant by the Last Judgment in the Word.

SPIRITUAL DIARY ¶ 4975; 5202

Commenting on Revelation 6:12, Swedenborg wrote the following about its imagery:

'Earthquakes' signify changes of state in the church, because 'the earth' signifies the church; and because in the spiritual world, when the state of the church is perverted anywhere, and there is a change, there is an earthquake, and as this is a prelude to their destruction, they are in terror. For the [different kinds of earth] in the spiritual world are in appearance like [those of] the natural world; but as [they], like all other things in that world, are from a spiritual origin, therefore changes occur according to the state of the church among the inhabitants, and when the state of the church is perverted, they quake and tremble, yea, sink down and are moved out of their place.[7]

[7]*Apocalypse Revealed*, ¶ 331, tr. John Whitehead, 2nd edition (West Chester, Pennsylvania: Swedenborg Foundation, 1997).

When we feel the ground of reality shifting beneath our feet, we may re-examine our basic values and understanding of life. People who experience earthquakes are psychologically, not just literally, shaken up; they often feel that they are being "spoken to." In disasters like this, inner insecurities are aroused, completely out of proportion to the physical damage that is actually happening. We cannot evade the fact that we are spiritual beings and that the language of the spiritual world lies within us, ready to respond to messages couched in its own terminology.

Rational argument can help now. A major clue to the existence of an inner sense to the old predictions was the presence of physically impossible events that do make much better sense when taken spiritually. For example, about the last days we read in Matthew 24:29–31 that

> *Immediately after the tribulation of those days the sun shall be darkened, and the moon shall not give her light, and the stars shall fall from heaven, and the powers of the heavens shall be shaken. And then shall appear the sign of the Son of man in heaven; and then shall all the tribes of the earth mourn; and they shall see the Son of man coming in the clouds of heaven with power and great glory. And He shall send forth His angels with a trumpet and a great sound; and they shall gather together His elect from the four winds, from end to end of the heavens.*

The Second Coming of the Lord was supposed to be visible to everyone, despite the fact that the surface of the planet curves away from any point in space, making events at that point only locally visible. And the stars were to fall to the earth, when they are far larger than the planet and would much more likely make the planet fall toward them. Today we know that the stars are so far away that this one event, the fall of the stars, would take eons to complete, and the earth would have been destroyed by the first star, or sun, to hit it. The description in Matthew is appropriate to its time, reflecting an older cosmology in which people believed that they were alone among the stars. But now we have to wonder about the implied destruction of other (possibly inhabited) planets and the strong possibility that a literal tradition in millenarian churches has simply pushed itself and the cosmos out of shape, solely in order to keep the Bible literal.

If earth is not the planet Earth but the earthly realm of human consciousness and our mundane adventures—the "earth" that contrasts with heaven and the higher mind—then the fate of the universe is not an issue in Last Judgment prophecies. We need consider only the people who have caused such a state of inner deterioration. The curvature of the planet stops being a problem for similar reasons. The picture begins to look truly spiritual, not physical, and it thereby picks up much additional meaning.

The millennium in which the saved shall reign with God for a thousand years was for Swedenborg not a thousand-year period, but a state of conjunction with God. Linear time is not real to the spiritual world; such time is measured out only in the material realm. In the "other" world, only qualities or states of life and consciousness exist. The other world, as we put it here, is timeless. Events do continue, and simultaneity exists between the two worlds. But in a timeless environment the number of hours, weeks, or years that pass between any two events is meaningless.

Eons can pass in our world while someone in the other world finds life moving very normally over an apparently short period of time. The reverse can also happen. Swedenborg found that the higher a spirit is in heaven and the closer to God, the more time seems to be shortened, compressed into one moment comprising what we would recognize here as the present, along with portions of the past and future. To God, Swedenborg said, all three are completely and simultaneously present.

If God is only in the present, like ourselves, the present would be an absolute, containing everything that exists. However, God is not merely in our present, and therefore the present is not a stable quantity. It seems to be merely a way of talking about a state of consciousness and how it relates to other states of consciousness. Yet the drama of creation and its adventures is not therefore over for God—for eternity seen as a single moment is timeless, not transient.

From this perspective the term "a thousand years" has a cosmic ring to it, suggesting like good metaphor a timeless state of indefinite but not infinite duration rather than a calibrated period. It looks odd in any case, for it is unlikely that God would choose such an arbitrary period merely because it produced a round number and then count the years until it was finished. It would seem unlikely that the events of the apocalypse would, in their natural course, take intervals that precisely coincide with big round numbers on our calendar. That would imply that the calendar is governing the apocalypse rather than the apocalypse the calendar. Why should the thousandth year be any more significant than the thousand and thirty-first year? What has it got that the latter year doesn't? Only a certain picturesqueness. Picking a thousand-year interval seems more like something that Hollywood might do for some kind of dramatic effect.

"A thousand years" is such an impressive concept that it ends up as a way to refer to something numinous, grandiose, in its significance. The glamor of the idea overwhelms the math and becomes its central meaning. It is a period representing the presence of significance, a turning point. A change of consciousness and direction will occur in it, as if it made everything new or pushed events down a different and better path, bringing more life to those who go through it. At such points we all feel that our lives have been renewed or in some sense remade, and the past then seems very distant because it is no longer a part of our self. We may even say in ordinary metaphorical language, "Oh, I felt that way a thousand years ago."

A "thousand years," therefore, becomes a symbol of inner transformation. Swedenborg addressed this point in *Apocalypse Revealed* ¶ 855:

*I can assert that the angels do not understand any number naturally,
as men do, but spiritually [i.e., as a type of change of their inner
character or consciousness]; yea, that they do not know what a thousand years are, except that it is some interval of time, small or great,
which cannot be otherwise expressed than by some time.*

In other words, a literal millennium is not what angels think
about when the words "a thousand years" are used. Their perception is that a thousand of our years is merely small or
great, just some period of time, in which they would not pro-
fess much interest. But to them, in their experience of time,
it is a spiritual state of some large general value:

*[The angels] are surprised there, that, when the men of the church
have seen in the Apocalypse so many numbers, which cannot but signify things, they should still adhere to the conjectures of the . . . millennialists, by which their minds are impressed with vain things
concerning the last state of the church.*

APOCALYPSE REVEALED ¶ 842

For the saved to reign with God during this period is not
actually to reign with him, for that is impossible. Only God
can reign over anything. It refers instead to the state of conjunction with God that is built by a good life in service to him
and to which the lower self with its natural and mundane desires is now in subjection. Swedenborg says that those who
reign with God for a thousand years are those "who have been
already for some time in conjunction with the Lord and in His
kingdom" (*Apocalypse Revealed* ¶ 849). They have been prepared to rise into that state of greater spiritual realization and
balance once old obscuring evils and fallacies are singled out
and removed from the field of daily activity and consciousness. "Satan"—the metaphorical power of evil, is then impris-
oned for the thousand years—taken into custody, as it were
suppressed so that the embattled spiritual mind can emerge
and make its true claim over the field of conscious life. To

"reign with God" at this time is to be raised into this dominant state, after the storm of the preceding events, and be able finally to look down with a new wisdom at the many problems that life had presented and fully realize that a warmer perspective now explains one's existence. Obscurities and conflicts are now gone. A state of transcendence and fulfillment is experienced with no definite sense of material time.

After the removal of the faithful, or the spiritual mind, to a properly dominant position over the broad spiritual landscape, the release of Satan from prison to scheme and prowl about our day-to-day life again would only mean that satanic influences could now be exposed. In the following verses, he and his servants plot destruction, becoming more villainous than ever:

> But fire came down from heaven and consumed them, and the devil who had deceived them was thrown into the lake of fire and brimstone where the beast and the false prophet were, and they will be tormented day and night for ever and ever.

> Then I saw a great white throne and him who sat upon it; from his presence earth and sky fled away, and no place was found for them. And I saw the dead, great and small, standing before the throne, and books were opened.
>
> REVELATION 6:9–12

As Swedenborg explains in many places, evil must be allowed to come out in the open so that it can be recognized and rejected by all concerned. But this does not happen until a basic order is in place where high ideals are finally in a ruling position. Satan is loosed from his prison, and the result is an exposure of evil in its worst forms, with all polite disguises thrown away. That allows a final "judgment," or clarification of values, that we can see and accept, without having to contend with a confusing mixture of evil and good.

From this, we see that the apocalyptic drama is basically the description of a turning point in human consciousness, an inner reordering and transformation, though only in those who had remained able to recognize and receive it. More history always follows these great turning points, and the spiritual drama always continues, but with new resources.

New problems will plague us in the new era, and we will be often alarmed at the many hellish events that are happening now. But the critical consideration is whether or not we are aware of evil and care enough to do something about it. The great fault of old religious dispensations is that of the weakened conscience, not failure of power to defeat the world's evil. They were ineffective because they lost their sense of evil and became numbly unaware of its existence. Only good can recognize evil. The struggle to clean up our world against many different threats, even should the struggle ultimately fail, marks a vibrant religious age.

There is no recourse to an end of the physical world—no one will be able to change or repent, if that is what the last days or the millennium is all about. The literal and traditional version of it may cause people to give up on themselves and on each other, if only because they fear that God has, just at a time when it would be more spiritually effective to pull together. An inner millennium, however, is a healing and a continuation of life on a higher level. The spiritual millennium is hidden in the broad sweep of material history, a turning point that anyone who has the capacity to look inward at the character of his or her life and at a God of love will recognize.

aving a choice between literal interpretations and metaphorical or symbolic interpretations of apocalyptic visions makes a vast difference in the way we view our God and our spiritual lives. A problem with literal readings of catastrophic visions is that they present a *fait accompli:* there is really nothing left to do but run for the safe areas and be very scared. A more creative possibility is to contemplate that spiritual growth is to continue and that God, as Love itself and Wisdom itself, is passionately working to save or improve everyone he has created. Believing in a loving God, we should expect that he will keep creating people to love, not shut down history and cut off his own creativity.

Millenarian predictions must be delivered as they are actually experienced by psychics, for that is just honest reporting. But in accepting them as literal truth and refusing to interpret their symbols, we tacitly revert back to old ideas of a jealous God ready to visit divine justice *en masse.* God remains in most spiritual movements unclearly defined, undifferentiated from the Judaic or Old Testament image. Our saviors—the inspired, human leaders of our spiritual movements—are typically lesser beings of saintly inclinations. Even Jesus has occasionally been reduced to the status of a saint, rather than an emanation of God's true nature. Holy people attract our love, while we remain uncertain and fearful about the source of all goodness, God.

Such an attitude leaves religion headless, without an ultimate reason for maintaining itself. If its highest power is of uncertain sympathies—loving and forgiving one moment, vengeful the next—then the entire structure of spirituality or religion can collapse. We turn, instead, to human beings whose authority may be overruled by the next spiritual leader who captures our hearts. Some saint, prophet, *bodhisattva*, or avatar whom we admire for his or her solidity, patience, and virtue, who sees the good as well as the evil in individuals, may not have a lasting effect. If we are unable to bring a better sense of divine love to visions of the millennium, we deny ourselves happiness and inner fulfillment. For a God not in favor of happiness and inner fulfillment, unwilling to keep loving the human race, deters us from embracing spiritual truths and from seeking the highest good. Religion loses credibility if the God at the center of our faith is himself a liability.

BIBLIOGRAPHY

Bloom, Harold. *Omens of Millennium: The Gnosis of Angels, Dreams, and Resurrection*. New York: Riverhead Books, 1998.

Boettner, Loraine. *The Millennium*. Philadelphia: Presbyterian and Reformed Pub. Co., 1958.

Bryant, M. Darrol, and Donald W. Dayton, ed. *The Coming Kingdom: Essays in American Millennialism and Eschatology*. Barrytown, New York: International Religious Foundation, 1983.

Carter, Mary Ellen. *Edgar Cayce on Prophecy*. Edited by Hugh Lynn Cayce. New York: Hawthorn Books, Inc., 1968.

Cohn, Norman R. C. *The Pursuit of the Millennium: Revolutionary Millenarians and Mystical Anarchists of the Middle Ages*. Revised and Expanded. London: Maurice Temple Smith Ltd., 1970.

Erdos, Richard. *A. D. 1000*. New York: Harper & Row, 1988.

Finley, Mark A. *Discoveries in Daniel*. Siloam Springs, Arkansas: Concerned Communications, 1994.

Fontbrune, Jean Charles de. *Nostradamus: Countdown to Apocalypse*. Translated by Alexis Lykiard. New York: Holt, Rinehart, and Winston, 1980.

Garraty, John A., and Peter Gay, ed. *The Columbia History of the World*. New York: Columbia University Press, 1972.

Gould, Stephen Jay. *Questioning the Millennium: A Rationalists's Guide to a Precisely Arbitrary Countdown*. New York: Harmony Books, 1997.

Lorie, Peter. *The Millennium and Beyond: The Prophecies to 2016*. New York: Simon and Schuster, Labyrinth Books, 1993.

Marsden, George M. *Fundamentalism and American Culture: The Shaping of Twentieth Century Evangelicalism, 1870–1925*. New York: Oxford University Press, 1980.

Roberts, Henry C., ed. and trans. *The Complete Prophecies of Nostradamus*. Oyster Bay, New York: Nostradamus Co., 1982.

Sandeen, Ernest R.. *The Roots of Fundamentalism: British and American Millenarianism, 1800–1930*. Grand Rapids, Michigan: Baker Book House, 1978.

Sigstedt, Cyriel O. *The Swedenborg Epic: The Life and Works of Emanuel Swedenborg.* New York: Bookman Associates, 1952.

Sugrue, Thomas. *There is a River: The Story of Edgar Cayce.* New York: Henry Holt & Co., Inc., 1942.

Thurston, Mark A. *Visions and Prophecies for a New Age.* Virginia Beach, Virginia: A.R.E. Press, 1981.

Weber, Timothy P. *Living in the Shadow of the Second Coming: American Premillennialism, 1875–1982.* Chicago: University of Chicago Press, 1987.

INDEX

Divine, the, 106, 109–110, 118,
126–127

E

"earthquakes," as signifying changes in
the church, 127–128
Edwards, Jonathan, 12
end of world, 4, 18. *See also*
Armageddon.
Enoch, 5
Episcopalian Church, 18
Erdos, Richard, 8
Evangelical Free Church, 19
evil, 25–26, 132–133
spiritual, 26
evolution, Darwin's theory of, 17–19

F

Federal Council of the Churches of
Christ in America, 18
First Presbyterian Church of New York
City, 18
Fontbrune, Jean-Charles de, 63
Fosdick, Harry Emerson, 18
Franz, E. W., 36
Fundamentalists, 13–26
Fundamentalist millenarians, 17, 24, 25

G

Galileo Galilei, 11, 45
General Association of Regular Baptists,
19
Genesis, book of, 7, 38
God, 6–7, 122, 126, 136
as possessor vs. source of love and
wisdom, 110–111, 135
Swedenborg on, 131
Gould, Stephen Jay, 8 (n.4)
Graham, Rev. Billy, 17, 21, 22
"Great Disappointment, The," 36
group consciousness, 102–103

H

Hegel, Georg, 9
Hippolytus, 6
Hobbes, Thomas, 9
Hodge, Charles, 15

Holy Spirit, 6–7
humanistic astrology, 61
Huxley, Thomas, 20

I

individuality and unity with others, 103
Infinite, creative power of the, 87–88
inner sense, 114
Inquisition, 123
Irenaeus, 6, 7, 12

J

Jehovah's Witnesses, 29–31, 34–36
Jesus Christ. *See* Christ
Joachim of Fiore, 8
John, book of, 22
Judgment, 7, 29, 36, 39–42, 89, 109,
127, 129, 132
by Christ, 3
Swedenborg on, 92, 117–118, 120
Jung, Carl G., 40, 59–61, 98

K

Kahn, David, 77
Ketchum, Wesley H., 72–74, 77, 79

L

Lammers, Arthur, 78
Laplace, Pierre Simon de, 11, 88
"last days," 14, 118
Last Judgment. *See* Judgment.
Layne, Al C., 68–70
League of Nations, 18
Locke, John, 9
Lorie, Peter, 45–49
love, 106, 135
self-sustaining, 109–110
Luke, book of, 32, 38
Luther, Martin, 44

M

Mabus, 46–47
Machiavelli, Nicolo, 9, 10
Martyr, Justin, 7
Matthew, book of, 37, 38, 122, 128
maya, 96, 111
Mead, Joseph, 12

religion. *See also* Bible; Christianity;
Fundamentalists; Jehovah's
Witnesses; Seventh-Day Adventist.
problems of, 136
science and, 90, 93
religious worship, as regeneration, 125
repentance, 123
Revelation, book of, 4–6, 27, 36, 38,
117, 124, 127
Rudhyar, Dane, 59, 61
Russell, Charles Taze, 30–34
Rutherford, Judge Joseph Franklin,
33–34

S

salvation, 123
Satan, 118, 131, 132
science, 10–12, 40, 85, 90, 99. *See also*
modernism; secularization of
society.
religion and, 90, 93
Scripture. See Bible
Second Coming, 3–4, 16, 24–25, 27,
37, 80–81, 95, 116, 124, 128. *See
also* apocalypse; Christ; Judgment;
millennium.
signs of, 38
secularization of society, 10. *See also*
modernism; science
self-consciousness, 102
Seventh-Day Adventists, 27–31, 37–39
"signs of the times," 38
soul
ephemeral, 89
nature of, 88–89
Southern Baptists, 18
spirit, 94, 102–103
spiritual experience, 97, 98
spiritual indifference, 124–125
spiritual rebirth, millennium as, 29, 37
spiritual trends, importance of, 53
spiritual world, 75, 91–92, 94,
101–107
experienced as reflection of
observer's state of mind, 108
as group consciousness, 102

relation to material world, 98, 100,
107
Swedenborg on, 126–127
Storrs, George, 30
Student Volunteer Movement, 17
subconscious mind, 75
Swedenborg, Emanuel, 46, 113, 123,
125
on the apocalypse, 107
on Bible, 113–117, 121, 124, 127
on Christianity, 117, 122, 124, 125
on God, 131
on humanity, 119
on individuality, 103–104
on the Infinite, 87–88
interpretation of spiritual imagery,
108
life history, 85–87, 89
spiritual crisis, 89–90
on millennium, 95, 116, 117, 129
on natural vs. spiritual thinking,
96–98
on "past-life memories," 91–92
psychic abilities, 90–91
psychology of, 75
reinterpretation of Last Judgment,
92
science and, 85, 90
as spiritual scientist, 91
on spiritual world, 91–92, 94,
101–110, 126–127
writings of, 96
Apocalypse Revealed, 117,
130–131
Arcana Coelestia, 116–117
Doctrine of Sacred Scripture, 116
Heaven and Hell, 101
*Last Judgment and Babylon
Destroyed*, 117, 119
Principia, 87–88
symbolic nature of universe, 61
syncronicity, 59–60

T

Tertullian, 6
Three Worlds and the Harvest of This World
(Barbour), 31

truth, 116, 126–127
Truth Shall Make You Free, The, 34

U

unconscious mind, 75
Ussher, Bishop James, 31
utopian world, change to, 5, 6, 28–29.
    See also City of God

W

Warfield, Benjamin B., 15
Watch Tower Society, 33–36

Watchtower Bible and Tract Society, 30
Wendell, Jonas, 30
Wheaton College (Chicago), 17, 21
White, Ellen Harmon, 36, 37
White, James, 36, 37
wisdom, 109–110
"Word," the, 113–117
world, as cyclical, 6
world wars, 33, 48
World's Christian Fundamentalist
    Association, 17
worship, as regeneration, 125

Chrysalis Books

ILLUMINATING THE WORLD OF SPIRIT

Seeing Through Symbols: Insights into Spirit
Carol S. Lawson and Robert F. Lawson, Editors

"The great spiritual adventurers found the whole of creation and every part of it symbolic." —From the Foreword by Wilson Van Dusen

Lavishly illustrated short stories, essays, and poems show how symbols act as conduits to bring us understanding and enrichment. The contents are arranged to draw us through a "looking glass" into an expanding universe of symbol, from which we step back to a different starting point, renewed as if waking from an illuminating dream. This book is the fifth in the Chrysalis Reader Series, literary collections that explore a different spiritual theme in each annual publication. 0-87785-229-4, pb, $13.95

A Psychology of Spiritual Healing
Eugene Taylor

"This book will make the great healers throughout history stand up and cheer. . . . [I]t is a clear vision of the future of healing." —Larry Dossey, M.D.

Eugene Taylor uses psychology, the world's religions, and his own interior exploration to propose a dynamic psychology of immediate, spiritual experience that is self-healing and transformative. Drawing from transcendentalism and the psychological experiences and theories of William James, Emanuel Swedenborg, Mircea Eliade, Carl Jung, Victor Frankl, and Abraham Maslow, Taylor explores the relationship between beliefs and health, religion and consciousness. 0-87785-375-4; pb, $14.95

Light in My Darkness
Helen Keller / Ray Silverman, Editor

". . . an inspiring picture of this remarkable woman's affirmation of the power and triumph of the spirit." —*New Age Retailer*

Helen Keller's optimism and service to humanity were inspired by her readings of Emanuel Swedenborg, whose insights were her "strongest incitement to overcome limitations." This is Keller's 1927 spiritual autobiography, revised and enlarged with her letters, speeches, and other writings. She calls Swedenborg's theology "an inexhaustible wellspring of satisfaction to those who lead the life of the mind." 0-87785-146-8, pb, photographs, $11.95

The Last Judgment in Retrospect
Emanuel Swedenborg
Edited and translated by George F. Dole

In 1757, in one of his many visits to heaven, Swedenborg saw a startling event: the Last Judgment, which took place in the heavenly realm. This remarkable book stresses God's mercy rather than the traditional vision of wrath and retribution: Swedenborg asserts that biblical prophecies must be read symbolically to understand their true meaning. This work affirms the continuation of life on earth, the triumph of good, and eternal salvation. 0-87785-176-x, pb, $9.95

Heaven and Hell
Emanuel Swedenborg
Translated by George F. Dole

"One of the most fascinating guides to other worlds in the Western spiritual canon." —Gary Lachman, *Gnosis*

First published in 1758, *Heaven and Hell* is a treasure for all who seek to know of life after death. Dole's translation makes Swedenborg's most important work both accessible and compelling. Swedenborg describes heaven, the world of spirits, and hell, and explains their meaning and relationship to earthly lives in the "natural" realm. Well-delineated chapters help readers explore their questions and learn why choices in this life affect their realities in the next. 0-87785-153-0, pb, $10.95

Emanuel Swedenborg: A Continuing Vision ▪ SALE
Edited by Robin Larsen, et al

". . . the richest book for the dollar we have seen in 14 years of reviewing books for BRAIN/MIND BULLETIN." —Marilyn Ferguson, author of *Aquarian Conspiracy*

This handsome, pictorial biography of Emanuel Swedenborg also presents essays by such prominent contributors as Jorge Luis Borges and Czeslaw Milosz. Their essays testify to Swedenborg's genius and to the vitality of his continuing vision.
0-87785-137-9, pb, $39.95 29.95; 0-87785-136-0, hc, $49.95 39.95

To order these and other books or receive a free catalog:
Individuals: Call (800) 355-3222; Fax (610) 430-7982;
Web Site: www.swedenborg.com.
Swedenborg Foundation Publishers
PO Box 549, West Chester, PA 19381

Booksellers: Call (800) 729-6423
SCB Distributors • 15608 S. New Century Drive, Gardena, CA 90248